A Necessary Clearing

By
Amber Howard

Cover Design: Amber Howard & Carlos Xavier
Cover Photography: Howard Hill
Back Cover Photography: IVA Enterprises

Copyright © 2017 Amber Howard

A Necessary Clearing / Amber Howard – 1st edition

ISBN-10: 1545066728
ISBN-13: 978-1545066720

DEDICATION

To the little girl in me, that no longer has to go without full support.

CONTENTS

ACKNOWLEDGMENTS

Thank you to all of the people in my life;

who through both positive and negative situations,

have shown me what internal balance truly means.

Also a huge thank you to the people quoted in this book,

and more, whose work and insights

have been an immense help to me.

And finally, a deep thank you as well, to my Mom:

for her love, friendship, help and support;

most especially within these last eight significant years for me.

A Gift

What Brilliance! What Light!

To be able to move beyond the Night

Into the warm glow of the Sun!

A True Gift.

To Stand -

Arms outstretched,

Chest forward,

Eyes to the sky...

And know, down to the very depths of you -

There is no reason to run...

No reason to hide,

Or for snide judgments,

Cloaking despair,

Giving into the fear that impairs,

The Self Protection, always there,

Creating for some, too strong a gloaming glare,

3

To stay open...

Holding every moment hostage.

NO! It is the glow into which we all can turn and go!

Careful to hold onto the lessons of the night

But steadily,

And pointedly,

Continuing to move into the bright arc of the beam.

To a better tomorrow.

An end to useless sorrow, grudges and regrets.

And turning instead,

To the beauty in the experiences you haven't yet met.

Knowing that even Alone,

You have the Universe's forward moving energy,

Right along with you,

Guiding you,

Directly under your feet.

Containing the larger lessons,

Strong opportunities,

Important relationships,

And inevitable successes,

That you are sure to meet.

It is your time -

Your life, your love, your joy, your thoughts, your choice -

Within you...Within all of us...

Within our ability to make our individual journey complete.

~Amber Howard

Introduction

Hello,

I am sharing my story and my thoughts on what I have understood from my life so far, because I truly want to help people. I am hoping that you can really take in my story and absorb the overall message, in order to avoid making any of the same mistakes I have made. I want to help you to live your life to the fullest and to avoid getting stuck in any situations where you find that too much time has gone by in negativity.

Life is a gift.

However, there are definitely times though, when it can seem and feel like the opposite. But even in times of great pain and darkness, there is always light. (Yes, I know that kind of statement can sometimes make people cringe with irritation but it really is true).

I want to help people fully understand that message. That it isn't just some nice thing that people say to try to make people feel better. And I'm hoping that hearing about some of the things that I have gone through, will help you to not just understand it intellectually, but to really feel that "light" deep within yourself as well, no matter what is happening in your life, at any given time.

We are completely in charge of our own happiness. It is something that comes from within us, not from outside of us. And that happiness cannot exist and thrive in your life, if you are not capable of unconditionally loving yourself.

Now, I'm not using the word, "unconditionally", as in making excuses for the negatives within you, or for any weaknesses, or being in a state of ignorant avoidance, or worse – in a state of self-entitlement. No. I am talking about unconditional love that is personally responsible, personally accountable, healing and pro-active.

We came from love and we will pass away from this lifetime back into love. But that love is also here in this lifetime, if we choose it. We just have to be able to open ourselves to it. I have seen this and experienced it very clearly and would like to serve as just one example that will hopefully help you to feel motivated for finding more balance in your life…and the active Self-Love it takes to achieve it.

So I will start by talking about my past. I didn't realize how much of a prisoner within myself that I was living; stuck deep within the fear and illusions of my own thoughts and emotions.

~

Chapter 2

<u>Past To Present</u>

The most formative years of a child's life are in the first 5 years. And if there is trauma suffered within those years, it leaves a deep psychological impact on the person's life for years and years to come, if it is never able to be addressed and healed. And unfortunately I am one of those people that suffered trauma and did not understand how to heal from it. It has taken me my life so far, to understand just how deeply everything has run, in order for it to be truly seen and nurtured toward healing.

From the time that I was a very young child, (from what I can remember at age 2 and up), I used to constantly have nasty nightmares. It has felt like I came into this world even, with a lot of baggage. I would have a lot of nightmares that were violent and filled with cruelty, even before I could ever understand what any of it was. I used to dream about be-headings a lot. And later began to wonder if that was how I had died in my previous life, along with people that I had cared very deeply about.

Despite this, I was a considerably out-going child. My mom says that she used to get scared with me, because I would just run right over and sit on someone's lap and strike up a conversation with them, without a second thought, before she ever realized I was gone.

But all of that changed at age 4, when I had three very traumatic, abusive situations happen to me.

One was involving a new pre-school that I had just started attending. The pre-school teacher got angry at me during story time, because I had said something to the girl next to me and we had both laughed. She was thinking that I was making fun of her in some way, or of her story telling choices. I hadn't been. I had made a comment about the story itself; something that I had liked about it and had thought was funny and shared it with the girl next to me. But this teacher flew off the handle, started screaming at me and made me get into a large toy chest that sat at the back of the classroom. I remember it had an exaggerated key hole in the front of it. She made me shut myself into the box. I was hysterically shocked and crying. I was deeply afraid of the dark too, because of my constant nightmares and was terrified to get into the chest. She made me. And I can still remember to this day, looking through the large keyhole of the chest at the girl that I had made the comment to, and her extremely sad face looking back at me. I was still crying and she yelled at me once to stop, followed by another time where she angrily walked over and hit the box and threatened me to stop crying. I became much more quiet. I was in there for the remainder of the length of the story.

Afterward, when I could come out again, the teacher was cold to me and I was in shock. When my mom came to pick me up, I couldn't get out of there fast enough and became hysterical all over again when telling her what had happened once we were in the car. My mom went back in to talk to her. Of course the teacher lied. She even went so far as to say that I not only had made it all up but that I was a problem child; and that she was walking a dangerous line with me because if she gave into me now about this "made-up" situation, then I would have her in the palm of my hand.

I never went back there again. But my parents did not push anything about getting her fired. I never showed it but this really upset me. And I always felt like the whole incident, although deeply traumatic to me for years to come, was just glossed over and "removed". But it was not "removed" for me inside.

*****

The second, was involving a family that had just moved in next door. There was a girl there, who was only seven, who upon our first meeting did some sexual things to me and told me that if I ever said anything to anyone, she knew that she could convince them that I had been the one to do them to her…that that is what she would definitely say. I was heavily traumatized by this encounter with her for many years to come.

I never told anyone about it for a very long time…at first, because her coldness when she said it, made it very clear that she meant what she had said about blaming me and I believed her…but later, because of all of the typical emotions that come with a situation like that. I didn't really know how to talk about it.

But what complicated things too, is that the encounter created an interest in sex that should never be put into someone's head that is so young. By the time I was seven or so, I had discovered masturbation. Not that I had any full understanding of everything really, but enough understanding. But like so many other households, I was not in a situation where I could talk about it. All of it was deemed something "wrong" and shameful to do and to discuss.

I became someone that masturbated often but yet felt shame, confusion, guilt and embarrassment about it too. I felt that there was something wrong with me. I didn't understand, until I was older, that what I was doing was a way of trying to comfort myself from the things that were happening around me and the difficult emotions inside of me. I didn't have an outlet, so this had become one outlet…even though a very damaging one to me, since I didn't understand it and had so much negativity surrounding it.

And of course it wasn't until I was about 13 or so, that I understood that she had obviously been sexually assaulted herself and was acting out. But when you are only 4 years old, and have no idea what the hell is going on, or how to react to it, it can drastically traumatize you and did with me. I walked away from the first two instances with the very clear knowledge that nobody can ever truly protect me from anything and that you can never know how someone is going to be toward you.

*****

The third traumatic experience at age 4, was something I ended up doing to myself. I had always loved performing. I had a good singing voice. And I wanted to display and share it. After that horrible pre-school incident that I had had, my mom took me out of that pre-school and I started going to the pre-school that was run by our church instead.

During the holidays, they had asked for volunteers to do a singing performance of a few songs in front of the church-goers. I was excited to volunteer and asked to sing "Silent Night". I could sing it well. There was another girl, who often treated me badly and was always fighting to be the center of attention that was going to sing another song, but was irritated at me that I was getting to sing "Silent Night" because that was the song that she wanted to sing. The day of the performance came and I was terrified. And at the last moment, I chickened out and that girl jumped right in to sing the song, feeling so happy and "better than". And I walked away that day feeling so defeated and angry at myself. So much so, that I hated myself. And it made a drastic negative impact on me to come, from that day on. I would go on to have other experiences just like that one, through-out my life. The fact that fear and a lack of self-worth was standing in my way, was succeeding in making me lose faith and love in myself...which only made it much easier for outside influences with people and situations to make me feel less-than and unworthy as well.

Of course I didn't understand this at the time but the combo of all three experiences were leaving me feeling like nobody can really help me, or protect me from anything and I can't even seem to help myself.

I have always been a deeply sensitive person and unfortunately, if not taught how to protect yourself and to have balance and a strong loving foundation within yourself as a child, or even as an adult, you can end up with a huge target on your back. The reason being, because people, when not in balance themselves and see someone else in a weak or self-defeating state, it triggers any time within themselves that they have felt that way, or have been in that state. So, depending on how much baggage of their own they carry about such things, then they don't want to see it or be around it and they will often put down, shun, or attack that person for it. Again, not understanding it at the time, I was building that kind of target onto my back with the weight of the emotional difficulties, fear and confusion that I was carrying within me.

With more negative experiences piling and no outlet, or any understanding of how to protect myself, I learned to go much more into myself than I used to be. I stopped expressing myself quite as much, a little more and more over the years. And at certain times would become a doormat for others, because I was valuing them over myself…wanting to be liked…and not wanting anyone else coming at me in any way. I just wanted love and equality coming toward me but did not have the strength within myself, or the understanding of how to reinforce it. I began to overcompensate toward others at times, in order to try to keep things peaceful and fine for them, but it would often be at my expense. And in those situations, people often become abusive toward you anyway.

There was a family member that I deeply loved and often wanted to spend time with, that is a good example of this. There was a five year age difference, with them as my senior, so that didn't help things either. But this family member had resentment toward me, for a lot of reasons that didn't have anything to do with me, (not that I understood that back then). At the time, I just wanted this person to love and like me and to spend time with me. For their own reasons, they would often pick on me and shun me from being included in what they were doing. I understand that this happens a lot with kids. But I can say that this did have a very big painful affect on me throughout the years.

They knew I was a sensitive person too and knew that I could not control my emotions. So it became entertaining to them to upset me, hurt my feelings, and/or piss me off. And it was a special bonus for them, if I got into trouble for it with my parents, (by fighting, or being emotional, when it wasn't something that anybody wanted to "deal with"). This person would often purposely exclude me from group games, etc., and treat me as if I wasn't old enough, good enough, etc., to be a part of things. And if my parents made them let me join, it didn't help anything, because I knew they didn't want me there and they would make it known.

I remember often feeling so incredibly ragingly angry at times and also so deeply hurt. I didn't understand why they were so cruel to me. I hadn't done anything to them. I loved them. And I wanted to get along with them. So, why? ...

By the time I was around 10 years old, I had some more experiences that dug very negatively into my psyche.

I had a close friend, that I had been friends with for a number of years by that point, ask me over one night to spend the night. Nothing unusual. But that night, I had gotten up in the middle of the night to use the restroom. And I don't know why I made this decision, because I hadn't made it before while not at home but I was still struggling with sexuality and everything that had happened before and I decided to masturbate. Unfortunately, my friend's younger brother ended up waking up and caught me doing it. I was so mortified and I was scared he would say something. The next morning was extremely awkward. And sure enough, he did end up saying something to them later, when I wasn't around. Their parents ended up getting into a massive argument with each other in their bedroom over it. We could tell very clearly that they were arguing but thankfully could not make out a lot of what was being said.

Afterward it was clear that their dad had been arguing for me and their mom against me. She couldn't even look at me for long and when she did, I could have dropped dead on the spot from the coldness and disgust coming from her eyes.

I can remember getting a call at home from my friend, very soon after that day, where she told me that her mom had said she could no longer be my friend. I can't even begin to describe the pain, shame, self-disgust, unworthiness, embarrassment and horror I felt from that phone call. I barely had any words. I just basically said, "ok", and hung up.

My mom asked me what happened and I could never tell her. I remained vague and distant about it.

*****

That year as well, we had a fund raiser for school where we were selling things like stationery, stickers, pencils and pens, etc. I always loved all that stuff so I was excited about selling it. But I had fear and anxiety about having to walk around the neighborhood, knocking on doors, and trying to sell the stuff. I wanted my parents to help me and do it with me. My dad wasn't available to and my mom had said that it would be a good experience for me to do it myself. It took me a number of days to get myself to do it but eventually on a weekend, I did it.

Before that point though, the only thing I had ever sold was a little bit of candy for sports. And that is very straight forward. But this was different. It was an odd situation, because the person was paying upfront.

I finally got up the courage to take orders. But the whole time I was taking them, I kept feeling like something was nagging at me. But I just kept pushing it away. My main focus was on interacting with people and trying to talk about what was available in the catalog. By the end of the few hours that I had gone door to door, I had made a decent amount of money and a lot of people had ordered a lot of items.

I still had that nagging feeling with me though, when I went to school and turned the money and the orders in. And it wasn't until I had the large package of everything with me at home and was thinking about passing everything out, that it hit me, HARD. Yes, I had had the order sheet with all of the orders on them but I had not put down which house had ordered what! I went into a panic. I was SO UPSET at myself. I felt horrible, scared and nauseous and like a complete idiot that couldn't do anything right. I didn't know what to do.

All of the orders just sat in my room for many, many days. I couldn't stand looking at them but I was frozen with the whole thing. My mom said that I was just going to have to go around to the houses with the stuff and explain. But I didn't know how I was going to do that and the thought crossed my mind too that people might not take only what they ordered. I could never remember what everybody ordered, or which houses had ordered something exactly, so how was it going to help?

In the end, I never ended up going to the houses. I felt like a thief. And I know that plenty of the people in the neighborhood remembered that I had come to the house, taken their money but did not deliver their orders. Nobody said anything to me but they didn't have to. I felt lower than low and embarrassed in the extreme. I used to play outside all the time but after that, stayed inside much more, for a very long time. It was truly a hellish experience.

*****

Also in that same year when the new school year started, I was starting junior high. It was a drastic change from grade school; a big transition. But I liked the idea of having a variety of teachers and different classes to go to and I liked having P.E.

But socially, the transition was massive and it seemed like I hadn't gotten the memo. At that time, I had always been a big tomboy. I would even get mistaken for a boy at times, which I hated and found incredibly embarrassing. But oddly enough, I stubbornly would not change my look because of it. It was the feeling of wanting to change things when I wanted to change things, not because other people wanted me to, or didn't understand it. But it still was very difficult for me.

But when junior high started, it was like all the girls suddenly became extremely girlic; much more into fashion and makeup and putting themselves out there more. I would wear a tiny bit of makeup but it was always very light colors and barely-there shimmer, nothing massive. And my fashion style was non-existent. I wore plain color, or music t-shirts and jeans a lot. Had very short hair, where most girls had long hair. And I tended to go baggy, not figure flattering.

And looking back now, I know that, yes, I was very athletic and into all kinds of things that may not have seemed so stereotypically "feminine". But I know that a big part of the reason why I dressed in tomboyish clothes and baggie shirts, was because of everything I had been through. I wasn't ready to be noticed in that way yet. And by age 10, I was one of the fastest developing girls in my school. I had gotten teased in 5th grade for having to wear a bra already and I hated it. When you are struggling with feelings of shame and confusion surrounding sex and your body, it does not make you want to get dolled up and be any kind of center of attention, that's for sure.

My social situation at that point was difficult. I had just lost a close friend and I had had another so-called friend (who always treated me badly, so I can't really strongly use the word "friend"), that was going to be going to my school. During the first week, I noticed that she had really started to put in focus and effort to be popular and always stylish. And she, very quickly, was shunning me.

And eventually one day at lunch, I had gone up to her to talk to her about something and when she saw me coming, I could see her saying things to the other girls about me. She was being very obvious about it and laughing. When I approached her, she stood up from the table and purposely loudly started to express all of the horrible things she thought and felt about me: that I was "manly", that I had no fashion sense, that I was awkward and not good enough to hang around her and her new friends. Some of them laughed. Some of them, I could tell, felt horrified for me. I had no words, once again, in a moment like that. I just wanted to get out of there. I can't even remember if I said anything. I just remember standing there being made fun of and not knowing how to react. I just wanted to disappear.

Since that was the start to my junior high experience, I don't think it is a stretch to say that the three years I was there, was very difficult for me. I would be involved in some social situations here and there with people but I didn't have any real solid friends at school at that time. And I was talked about behind my back.

I remember there was one point where two girls, who I think just felt sorry for me, tried to befriend me. I appreciated it. But unfortunately I was so down, and had gone into myself so much, and felt so awkward, that it was very difficult for me to do anything about it. They ate lunch with me for a while. They would try to make conversation with me. We would talk a little bit but mostly it was the two of them talking to each other. And eventually, (I can't really say that I blame them), they decided they wanted to just be away from me.

Of course it hurt and was embarrassing and all kinds of negative emotions. But by that point, I just wanted to disappear. So I wasn't functioning socially well at all. Instead, I would continue to focus on my homework and get good grades, I played soccer outside of school and liked it. I had always liked dance too and had taken classes. These were practical things that I was interested in, that I could focus on and did not have to think about myself much while doing them.

But I was absent A LOT during junior high because it was always so difficult for me to be there. I spent most lunches alone, just eating and walking around. There was a big grass field at our school and if the weather was ok, I would just eat and walk out there. Or I would find a place to sit that was away from most people and just pass the time until lunch was over.

I felt extremely lonely and that inner feeling of being "wrong" at my core, was constantly with me. I didn't know how to change anything. I felt lost and hopeless. But I still just kept functioning at least, with school, etc., as I knew I needed to.

And I remember that on the last day of eighth grade, a girl I didn't know well, but knew that she had become friends with the two girls who had tried to befriend my before, came up to me and told me that those girls asked her to tell me that when we started high school, they didn't want me around them. In that moment, I felt a mix of emotions. I was hurt and embarrassed of course. And I was irritated that they had sent this girl to say something to me, instead of saying something themselves. But I was also very confused by this, because I hadn't talked to them in quite a while and had had no intention of doing anything with them anyway. I already knew that I had handled everything horribly and they wanted nothing more to do with me. So, why now? Why, at all?...

I was not looking forward to high school then, of course. I was dreading it over the summer. I had just pretty much given up in a social sense with school and just felt very raw and low.

But happily when I started high school, I was relieved to reconnect with a friend that I had first met when I was very little and had had a close friendship with, off and on at various chunks of time in my life, up to that point. She was a year older than me. And during that first week of my freshman year we started talking again and began to eat lunch together. I can't describe the relief and happiness I felt. It was like a beacon of light that I had desperately needed. Her friendship helped me to feel at least a little bit "normal". We had also eventually made another friend at school that ended up eating with us at lunch time. A wonderful person that I wish we could have kept the connection with but unfortunately it did not happen. Even though I didn't mean to, I ended up hurting her feelings and messing up that friendship. And the friendship ended. I felt badly about it but also didn't know how to help it at all.

So by my senior year, with one friendship ended and the other friend still close, but a year older and graduated already, I was left once again just keeping to myself, for the most part. At lunch time I would eat and just do homework, or read a book for fun, if I didn't have any homework to do. I was still friends with my friend outside of school. But with school, I had no social life and did not participate in anything other than school sports. I was on the varsity team all four years in soccer and decided to do track a bit, on the off season at one point, to help stay in shape. But I was not involved otherwise. I had always loved theater and badly wanted to be involved in it but I just didn't have the confidence for it.

As you grow older in childhood, into teen years, everybody has all kinds of good and bad experiences. And I am no different. But I can

23

say that there have been a considerable amount of bad experiences. And the reason why I am making a point of listing the larger negative ones here for you, is because I want to show that every single one of them just kept piling on top of me. I understood it consciously to a point but not enough to really be able to do anything about it to stop it. I was carrying them all, like a weight, and would continue to. And it was drastically affecting everything in my life. Every instance, of not only someone dumping on me in the form of selfishness, judgment, cruelty, etc., but also any time I had gotten in my own way out of fear, stopped myself from shining in my full power and individuality, stopped myself from expressing myself completely, etc., were all adding to that negative weight. It had made me develop anxiety issues in certain social situations. Of course, over time, I eventually got very good at hiding it. But if you hide that kind of thing, then it can sometimes make you come off as aloof, cold, or leave people thinking that you are stuck up. So either way, you're screwed.

So as you can tell, I have never been the type of person that always has a bunch of friends. At best, a few deeply close friends and then the close relationships that I had developed with family and that was it. Not that I didn't want to be more social. I definitely did. I have always been a person that likes to get to know people and to understand them. But I didn't feel normal. I continually carried that heavy feeling around, that there was something "wrong" with me. Yes there were some things that I liked about myself, of course, but most of what was going on in my own head toward myself was negative. I felt uncomfortable in my skin but really wanted to change that.

I took some time off from school before starting junior college. Part of me was afraid to make that choice. But I knew I would go to college. I just needed a break from the social stress and just felt generally burnt-out. I did do some part time work a bit but wasn't sure what I ultimately wanted to do in life and I felt stressed about that.

During that period, like so many other teenage girls out there, when faced with difficulty, I developed an obsession with fitness and weight. I ended up developing an eating disorder for a short time. It's just another way of trying to have some control over yourself and your life, when deep inside you feel chaotic and down on yourself. The good thing in my case though, is that the issue didn't end up lasting all that long. I realized what I was doing to myself. I knew it wasn't healthy. And I started reading up on all kinds of food, health, fitness and psychology information to decide on the best way to approach changing things for myself. I had always loved being active. So I ended up really enjoying the process of researching it all and trying out different types of fitness and styles of eating, to find out what worked best for me. Loving fitness, psychology, food and cooking, made it all a positive experience for me in the end. It helped me to refocus myself on health, instead of mainly paying attention to my size or measurements.

I even got up the confidence to try out modeling a little bit. Eventually I went to San Francisco for agency open calls to see if I could get signed. I kept hearing the same things from them though: 'you have a great look but we already have someone that has that same "girl next door" look that you have. Maybe if you lose a bit more weight and change your look up in some way that makes you stand out more, we will consider you. Come back in a few more months when you think you are ready.' In fact one agency said exactly that to me but flat out told me they would sign me if I lost 10 more pounds and would agree to shave my head and focus on working an androgynous look. I had already gotten down to 120 pounds before that go-see and had practically killed myself to get there; (stupidly not thinking about the difficulty it would take to actually maintain a weight like that, when it isn't anywhere near natural for me). So I couldn't see how I could possibly lose 10 more pounds. Plus, I had already gone through all of those years of difficulty of feeling "manly" and having people mistake me for a boy and now this woman wanted me to deliberately go out of my way to do it again?!

I was very tempted, because I really wanted to model. I enjoyed modeling and found it to be fun and challenging. Anything that forced me to be the center of attention was a challenge for me. And I also liked truly trying to create something that had a message to it, or some artistic beauty to it, in some way. So, honestly, if this person had said they would have signed me at the weight I was already at but just wanted me to shave my head, I would have said yes. I think I would have been horrified by it, but I would have done it. It was the lower weight that I knew I just couldn't do though, so I had to say, "Thank you but no, I literally can't."

And after that experience I got myself back up to a much more comfortable and healthy 130-135 pounds. If modeling through an agency meant having to practically kill myself to do it, then I guess it just wouldn't be in the cards for my life. I would model on the side for the fun of it. And if a paid gig ever came of it, great. But that wouldn't be my focus. I would just continue to do it as a form of expression and a way to keep pushing myself. I was disappointed. But much smaller scale focused projects would just have to do.

Once I started junior college, I was in great shape and I was ready to get back to it all. I also was starting to feel better about myself and starting to get a little bit more confidence. Eventually I finally got up the nerve to sign up for theater classes and loved every bit of it. It scared the absolute crap out of me and I was hard on myself as usual, but I did really love it. The first time I auditioned for anything, I got chosen to be a background dancer. I didn't end up doing it though. I would try out for other things after that and not get called back. But I knew I was still just trying to find my way with acting. But eventually there was a teacher who believed in me and would cast me

27

in small roles in his shows. I was deeply grateful to him for this and the experiences helped me out a lot, both in terms of acting but also socially and internally. Eventually, after taking singing lessons from a wonderful teacher for a handful of months, I auditioned for one of his musicals and actually ended up getting cast in my first lead role. I was so excited and it was an amazing experience to be able to do that.

Even though my interests in junior college had been jumping around from psychology/counseling, to journalism, to nursing/veterinarian, I ended up making the very impractical decision to get a theater Bachelor's degree. I had been in junior college for a long time, 5 years total, while I explored all these options but chose a school with a strong theater program in Southern California and left home to go there.

Back tracking a bit though; during that junior college period of time, I met a guy that would become my first boyfriend. And we ended up staying together for 14 years from that point.

He is an amazing person with so many talents and strengths and a big heart. I cannot express how grateful I am, to have been able to have him in my life.

Towards the end of our time together as a couple though, I could see how, yes, there were a lot of pluses in our relationship, but the difficulties were huge ones. We were very different people and those differences could be strengths, or minuses, depending. But we did have some extremely similar problems. And when two people have similar problems that they are needing to get past, but are struggling to help themselves with them, then they aren't really able to help each other with them either. We had gotten to a place that was very stuck and we hadn't been able to move forward in a long time. I could also see how our relationship had become unhealthily co-dependent too and I wanted and needed that to change. I was wanting to change a lot of things for the better. I was wanting to work on myself and to figure out how to be happy and how to move forward in my life. So I left. And it was the hardest decision I have ever made in my life. I still loved him. We still had a deep friendship. There was no betrayal that had acted as a catalyst. But it was how stuck and held-back we both were, that made me feel it was absolutely necessary.

In the time that followed, I was deeply torn apart by it all. I questioned my decision. It had crushed me to make the decision. But I also noticed that, once living on my own, that I felt a sense of freedom that I had deeply been needing. I also noticed that it was like I had been with him for so long, that I didn't even fully know who I was anymore. I had met him very young and we had been together for quite a long time. There was a sense of independence and the ability to do things for myself and in my own way, make decisions for myself, be autonomous, that I had been needing for so long, because it hadn't existed together. I also knew that I had a lot of work I needed to do on myself. I needed to figure out how to be happy…and most importantly, how to be happy on my own. And I knew that he did as well. That we both needed time to grow and to get through some things on our own, as individuals.

I also wanted to pursue performing. I would go on to have some small personal successes but also a lot of times where my fear would continue to get in my way and make it difficult for me to proceed.

*****

But oddly enough, it has taken three of the most abusive situations I have ever endured in my life, that have happened over these last eight years, to slowly snap me out of where I had been at, helped me to see everything much more clearly, and helped me to move into a much more equality-enforcing, inner-power-driven, self-loving state of heart, mind and soul.

It will be difficult to explain the effects of these three situations though, as separate, because they all overlapped each other.

The first was with a person who, over time, would have some good intentions toward me, but the majority of it was always pulled toward themselves. In other words, anything they thought of, that they saw as being for my benefit and might be helpful to me, kept getting pulled into ways of helping themselves. So in the end, it was actually created in order to help themselves with things they wanted.

It was not there to help me, for me, and me only. And they would relentlessly push themselves at me, cross my boundaries and ignore my feelings, words and actions. I repeatedly showed how uncomfortable I was by their behavior, in all kinds of subtle and not-so-subtle ways...I ran the gambit of reactions and emotions with it. And eventually would sit them down and have multiple talks about it too. But regardless, they would repeatedly spin the reality of everything to tell themselves and act like they were doing me a favor and "helping" me...when really they were only trying to help themselves. And it only escalated more and more, until it exploded in me having to seriously fight back in major ways, draw a clear line in the sand, and remove them from my life in any major way...for my own health and well-being's sake.

I say all of this quickly. But this was actually over a very long period of time of their incessant pushing; a period of years, in fact. The constant stress and anxiety of dealing with that situation was incredibly traumatizing and taxing for me, because during the entire time, I was having to battle myself too. I was having to battle that ridiculously overly compromising, overly giving and overly nice side of me...the side that could feel pressured to say yes to something, even when I wanted and needed to say no, or just wasn't completely sure...the sides of me that didn't want difficulty, power battles and conflicts. But they were so pushy and so self-focused, that I had no choice. I was pushed into having to push back for myself, in all kinds of ways, over and over again, by their relentless tactics and their

31

inability to see how it was affecting me. It left me ranging all over the place in emotions and constantly trying to figure out a middle ground with them. But I could never find one, because they could never truly get into their head, the difficulty and the stress they were causing me. I had spent so much time feeling supremely angry, both at myself and at them, any time I gave them an inch and they would take a mile. And I massively resented them for it and was hurt by it. I would repeatedly, very openly, talk about it all with them. Many times not helping being emotional as I did so. I laid out everything I felt and was going through and kept trying to keep my extreme anger under control, because I was trying to have it come across as much of a mutual conversation as possible, but still make my points. I had developed a friendship to a point with them over time, even in spite of the difficulty. And yes, they could be helpful and well-meaning at times but it inevitably, more often than not, seemed to have an edge of doing something for me, to eventually try to receive something for themselves. I tried for a length of it, to keep the relationship in tact but just try to change it to be a much more healthy and balanced situation for me, with the freedom that I needed, so that I didn't keep feeling put upon by them.

But they would still keep pushing and trying to maneuver for themselves. So an end to that relationship was the only clear choice for myself. And I made sure to say EVERYTHING I felt, every aspect of what I had gone through and was dealing with as a result of their behavior, in the hopes that they would one day realize that they cannot treat people like that and make it ok for themselves. People cannot be maneuvered and used, like some kind of ego-trip, or a business deal where, "I am going to voluntarily do this for you and act like it is a favor, so that you will then do something I'm wanting you to do, or be, for me later." And they don't get to lie about their tactics and intentions to themselves, to make themselves seem like they are "helping" or "teaching" and being so supposedly elevated and wonderful by their actions, when it is clearly an illusion they are telling themselves in order to feed their own egos. People deserve a hell of a lot more than that. So when what they are trying to maneuver with and push for, fails…they only have themselves to blame, for being so incredibly self-centered. I was done, two-fold with them: Done with me being too nice and not having clear enough boundaries in place for myself; and done with anybody trying to push themselves at me and trying to use me for themselves.

******

The second person was far worse. Again, it overlapped what I was going through with the first person as well, which added to all of the difficulty. And this one is also the hardest situation to explain.

There have been 5 people in my life that, upon first meeting them, there was an instant, strong reaction to them for me; something that told me that they were going to be extremely important to me in some large way in my life. And that feeling hasn't been wrong so far.

33

This person was the fifth and the strongest I have ever felt.

I felt such a strong pull toward them that it was like a freight train had hit me. I was completely blown away by them and wanted to know more about them because of it. I strongly wanted to connect with them to understand where this feeling was coming from. However, the situation was difficult and complicated considering how we had met, because he was in the public eye a bit. And this was a man that did involve an attraction from me as well, even though I knew that wasn't the whole reason for the pull. But that did succeed in complicating things further, especially because they were already involved with someone else.

Normally, that would be enough for me to put them completely out of my mind and walk away. ... (I would be curious to know how many of you feel that that statement is an odd one. There seems to be a view in single society where if someone is dating or with someone, but yet not married yet, then they are somehow still "fair game." To me, I absolutely can't agree. Maybe it is because I haven't really ever been in the typical dating scene in my life much, so to speak, so I admit I am kind of odd in that respect. Or maybe it is just because of who I am? But I feel that if I have strong feelings/pull/attraction toward someone and they are involved with someone else, then I shouldn't have anything to do with them. It wouldn't be right. Out of respect for the woman that is involved with them.

And any time I have ever had those lines blurred in my past, which thankfully hasn't been often, has truly been excruciatingly painful for me. Plus, to be involved with someone who is involved or dating someone else, would make me feel like I am just another piece of candy in a candy dish. It makes me feel like I am being used. And I am not ok with that. And it is the same in reverse for me. That is exactly why I can't handle more than one person at a time. When people have ever overlapped in interest or feelings for me in my past, it has been like a huge painful weight put upon me. It makes me feel like a terrible person, or like I'm messing with someone, if I am "split" like that. So I have never been able to deal with those types of situations well. I have thought a lot about this type of thing over my lifetime and I just can't help how I feel. Some people have called me old-fashioned, or not relaxed enough, because of it. But I just can't sleep around or date around like that. It is too hard for me. At least I haven't been able to, in that sense yet...I don't know if that will ever change or not. I've been tempted to change it. I have had chances to change it. I even tried once and wish I never had. But I can't help how I feel. If I am into someone, I want to truly be able to see if it is a true connection, one-on-one. No games. I am someone that values intimacy and a real connection, over just having "fun").

But this was the first time I had literally been unable to completely back away, no matter how hard I tried. And it was also the first time I had ever experienced meeting someone, feeling so incredibly drawn to them, but yet having the experience draw out so many feelings of unworthiness out of me.

Now granted, I had already been walking around in my life struggling to be in my own full personal power. And I have had times when I would meet someone, be interested in them, but not be able to say much because of embarrassment, self-consciousness, whatever, sure. But this was very different. It was way more than that.

When I would try to talk to them, I felt like I shouldn't be talking to them, because my feelings were so oddly strong and yet they were involved elsewhere. They were overwhelming to me. But I also felt like I shouldn't be talking to them because I couldn't seem to come across as my full self. I had too much self-consciousness and fears in my way and I was still trying to get over everything else that had been going on in my life as well. I felt like I had too much in my way to be able to "be" me; what I needed and wanted to be.

They also ended up inspiring me in ways I had never experienced either. I had dabbled with writing when I was younger. I knew I could write and had dabbled in poetry too. But upon meeting this man, words and inspiration were bubbling out of me uncontrollably. Like a frightening "volcano", they would want to come out, when I would try to email them…even when I was trying to be respectful and hold back, I still ended up a much larger waterfall of words and information, than I had ever intended.

It was terrifying and overwhelming and I felt guilty and confused. I felt like an idiot. It was maddening. I have NEVER in my life felt that way with someone, to that extreme…not before it and not since. And I hope I never feel that way again, especially after the hell I went through with everything that followed in it.

Even though they had opened some type of floodgate in me and I was writing a lot of poetry at the time, my poetry was filled with a lot of negativity toward myself; mirroring everything that I was feeling. I eventually realized that he was on some kind of pedestal for some reason and I couldn't figure out why. Intellectually, it all didn't make complete sense to me. But my emotions were clearly running the show. It was splitting me in two.

We talked for a short while, back and forth. I really enjoyed talking to him and wanted to get to know him but it was very difficult for me, as I said. It didn't matter what the topics were. It was more the situation itself. I didn't know what to do about it.

Eventually, I tried to pull away completely…especially since it seemed to me that any feelings and interest were only one-sided. But when I tried to pull away, that was when the judgments and criticisms began from him; that became the beginning of a very long, drawn-out struggle between us.

He started calling me guarded, closed and rigid. I understood what he meant to a point, but he was misunderstanding the situation. And I had not had experience with any situation like this before, so I didn't know what to do about it. I didn't want him angry with me, or feeling negatively toward me, so I would try to explain why I felt how I felt. But of course, I wasn't saying everything that I was feeling toward him, because I didn't want to come across as a crazy person. But I was doing my best to explain anyway.

But the more I would explain, the more he would criticize me. And he would speak to me in such a careful and calculated way, that it always came across like his actions were showing that he was taking it personally and was disappointed by it, but yet his words were always so cold and portrayed a persona like he didn't care at all really, he was just trying to "help me" and felt like I needed a "correction". It left me feeling a mix of infuriated, confused, hurt and feeling bad about it, all at once.

A ridiculously long, painful, back-and-forth interaction ensued. And it only increased with that same careful tone from him. He spoke to me like I was beneath him and like he didn't care, but yet he started doing and showing things in his behavior and actions that said otherwise. To me, he seemed hurt by it. But it was all so confusing. I couldn't understand it. If he didn't care, then why was he reacting in these ways? I was just trying to talk to him about it, but there could never seem to be any real conversation on his end. And eventually it became obvious that he had such bad feelings toward me about it that it deteriorated into some kind of verbal and emotional game to him. But I wasn't playing any games. I was truly trying to talk about it all in a real way.

After a long battle with this and greatly against my own better judgment, I finally told him fully how I had been feeling about him, (which was incredibly difficult for me to do) and he reacted how I feared he would; like he finally got the ego-stroking that he had wanted. He had already basically known what the problem was (maybe not the full powerful extent of it, but the basic issue, yes); he had just wanted the satisfaction of hearing me admit it.

The whole experience was degrading for me and I was so incredibly outraged and hurt. I had felt like I had put so much of myself out there to him, just to even resolve the misunderstanding we were having, because even though I had felt anxious in talking to him and needing to pull back, I was having to do the exact opposite of how I felt, in order to try to resolve it and explain it all. It was EXTREMELY difficult and painful for me. But yet all he could do was "play" with me. He wouldn't treat me with respect or equality, no matter what.

Eventually it got to the point where it became an all out war.

Now, I was fighting for everything that I was and for what I knew I deserved…but yet was still trying to resolve the situation in some kind of mutual way. And the more I would try to talk about it, to understand why he was being the ways he was, etc., the more he would come down on me.

It eventually became outright abusive from him. He accused me of being manipulative and lying; he said that I was a horrible communicator that "danced around subjects"; that I was immature and awkward; that I was playing emotional games with him; and that I was desperate and needy; basically unattractive and beneath him in my long list of faults. It was obvious from some of his friend's behavior toward me, that he had been talking badly about me to them as well. And he was using social media and other outside actions, as a weapon and a game-playing tool, against me too.

At first, yes, it all destroyed me. I felt like I was the equivalent of dirt from this experience and was trying to resolve it. I have never cried so much in my life. Everything I had already had a hard time with, within myself, was being brought up all at once in one painful blow, in trying to deal with this experience.

But also, I felt at the time that, yes, I had wanted to have things be a REAL conversation. And I was desperately wanting to resolve things. And yes, I wasn't the smoothest person that ever lived, not by a long shot. But I wasn't doing any of the things that he was accusing me of. They were projections of what HE was doing to me! HE was the one that was playing games, manipulating, lying and slandering. And he was being "desperate" in plenty of ways by being massively controlling and judgmental – like he HAD to have his way in every way. And HE was the one who could not and would not communicate in a real way…who was "dancing around subjects." He would always flip and dump everything on me and never own everything he was feeling. And he was way more "guarded, rigid and closed", than I had ever been! I was the only one of us who was trying to be open and REAL. I ended up completely exhausting myself to the point of mental, emotional, physical and spiritual sickness. It took up a ridiculously long amount of time and I could not think of anything else.

Nothing I ever did or said was "ok". I was never allowed to be right or understood about anything. And if I tried to talk to him about his behavior, he would tell me I didn't know what I was talking about. Part of me felt like it was obvious what he was doing, but yet he would tell me I was crazy and that I was a terrible person and it always left me feeling like I couldn't trust myself. It was gaslighting tactics. He acted like he was trying to "help me" in some way, because I was so "out there" and supposedly "off the mark". And he treated me like his time and who he was, had more value than me.

And I find it ironic that he always had a way about him like, "put in effort for me, show me what you're made of, go out of your way for me." And if I didn't, that automatically meant there was something wrong with ME. But it's all so ridiculous because I HAD been putting in effort...so much so, it had practically killed me! He just couldn't see it! Because all he ever saw was his own negative ego-driven wants, needs and demands.

I found myself really looking at everything deeply and trying to share it with him. But the problem is, if you have the ability to own weaknesses, fears and issues within yourself that need to be addressed, but you are talking to someone who can't and won't do the same, then they only use your admittances against you as a weapon and say, "See? You're even admitting some wrong doing, so it is all you!" But worse than that, I was battling times where my own inability to trust myself was leaving me feeling like everything WAS my fault, and so I was taking too much responsibility for things that were NEVER actually my fault or my problem. So I was getting slammed from myself and from him.

At the worst point of it all, it did succeed in crushing me into a million pieces. It was the last straw for me and I ended up having a full breakdown. I wanted to just die...disappear. I remember there was a flight I had taken at one point during that time. And I remember looking out the window and feeling so tired, down to my very soul and thinking, "if this plane went down right now, it wouldn't even phase me. Everybody would be screaming and panicked and I would be completely silent and would feel nothing but relief. I just can't do any of this anymore."

I felt like I couldn't do anything right. I did question my sanity for a time. Because everything I would say, he would say the opposite. I was always said to be wrong. I questioned everything. I could barely function anymore. I ended up right back in that "just getting by" mode, reminiscent of grade school, of just going to work, trying my best to hide everything, do what I needed to do...go home, exercise, or do what was necessary...but inside, I was just chaos and pain and sadness. And where I had always had difficulty trusting people, after this experience, all of that fear became much worse for a long chunk of time, because I no longer could trust myself, let alone trust anybody else. I felt like I didn't know what to believe anymore. If someone complimented me, or a guy tried to show interest in me, I could feel myself actually getting angry toward them. It was like I had hit such a massive low and felt so ugly and horrible inside, that to hear complimentary words had become something I could not trust anymore and did unfortunately show it, on a couple of occasions. It made rage come out of me and want to push them away, because I couldn't trust anybody to be sincere. I was a ball of confusion, pain, rage and sadness. I cried more over that long period of time, than I have cried all together in my whole life. I had truly exploded and didn't know what was up or down anymore. This went on for a ridiculously long time...more time than I can even bring myself to admit here.

I just kept circling and circling in it all because my mind was telling me I was not wrong about everything that was happening and the tactics that he was using but yet I was having to battle my life-long negative thoughts about myself too. And emotionally, I felt drawn to him and the strong positives I had seen in him but was faced with the reality of the despicable ways he was treating me, mixed with the fears and mixed emotions I had toward myself.

It took me a LONG time to get there, but I realized eventually that all the problems with us were there because we were just toxically circling from each other's fears and lack of self-love, coming to the surface.

I remember very clearly one point where he said to me, "I'm not a sucker." It thoroughly shocked me to hear it, because I had never been trying to make him a sucker. Not in any way, shape or form. He was just projecting his own tactics onto me. And those words told me very clearly where he was at within himself and the level of fear and distrust he holds towards others too, to react that way. I have never been his enemy. He made himself my enemy and it never had to exist.

I will never forget too, one time when he said to me in disdain, (and always with that calculated language that never could admit anything), something like: "What does it say about you, Amber, that you feel as you do about all of this and see things as you do, but yet you still keep trying to talk to me about it all?" I will remember this question for the rest of my life because it is a perfect example of how backwards this thinking really is. And my response, summarized more shortly here, was something like, 'To truly care about someone, will never be a weakness. Caring about someone, trying to help them and trying to find a middle ground in communication will always be a strength. So I know the ever-present lowliness you are implying about me, by your question, but I completely disagree with you and know what is strong and what is weak. So what does it say about YOU, that you keep choosing to behave in these dishonest, cruel and avoidance-ridden ways? That is the real question here.'

There was also a point, more toward the end of the long battle that we had been having, that he actually said to me something like, 'actually Amber, I did care about you and was interested in you…but all of your faults and issues have destroyed it. I am doing myself a huge favor then, by staying away from you.' This was the first time he had ever said that he had been interested in me…and he said it like THAT. After all that time, of talking to me like I never mattered…for him to say those words was just more of the same cruelty and ridiculous need to try to be "better than". It actually made me bitterly laugh to hear it. He never ONCE showed any type of true caring toward me. All he ever showed was his demanding for "ego-feedings" and that I do, be, think and feel what he wanted, how he wanted it…that's it. It was all just more of the same deep projections and complete hypocrisy for him to say it, because I did

45

not destroy anything…HE DID. And he showed plenty of his own faults and issues in doing so. He acted terribly, over and over again, and yet could only ever blame me for it all, rather than actually doing the right thing toward me and toward himself, by dealing with himself and being honest and respectful.

I came to understand that the key was always in a person's intentions. Their intentions were always completely self-serving, for their own set of reasons, both offensive and defensive. My intentions had grown from being all about them at first, at the expense of myself, to truly fighting for myself as an equal, on up to really seeing all sides of things and wanting to try to settle things in a healing way, that could be mutual. I was trying to truly connect with them to end the conflict and I wanted to help us both. I did not resort to their tactics in trying to do anything, even though I had been in the depths of hell from this situation and had so much immense rage and pain from it all, that it was hard to control my temper. But mostly I just felt an extremely large amount of sadness and disappointment that this person could not, and would not, hear me or meet me in the middle with anything. And they could not understand the larger picture.

Around and around…

This situation was the catalyst that really got me delving incredibly deeply into my childhood and on up to the present day, so that I could look at all of the patterns I was seeing from myself. The ways he was treating me was making all of my past experiences volcano up out of me, to have to address them. I could see that I have spent my life basically being abusive to myself too, beyond what others had been doing to me, simply because I didn't know how to love myself. I had been wrongly believing the instances of cruelty and negativity that had happened to me, when I had never needed to. I had been living from a place of thinking that if someone treated me badly and it was allowed to happen, then it must be largely my fault. I had been taking everything wrongly onto myself, throughout my life. But I had never deserved it!!!!!

I spent a lot of time, then, looking for answers. Beyond delving into myself and analyzing my actions, reactions, thought patterns and triggers, I was also reading anything and everything I could find that spoke to me. I read the absolutely wonderful Wayne Dyer's books and watched many of his talks; Took in books and talks from Anita Moorjani, who had a near death experience from cancer and was thankfully able to come back to share her experiences with us and talk about the importance of self-love; Books and talks from Joel Osteen; Books and talks from Louise Hay; Kyle Cease, Steve Maraboli and Bryant McGill; many psychology journals, philosophy, astrology, poets, quotes; and the absolutely amazing works of Osho, a man that I cannot possibly recommend to you all enough, along with everybody else I have mentioned here. (PLEASE read Osho's book called "Courage: The Joy Of Living Dangerously"; so much beauty and truth in those pages!).

I was delving deeply within all of these people's wonderful, helpful work, mixed with my own work on myself, and the incredibly amazing help and support of my Mom, who REALLY stood by me through it all, especially through these last 8 hardest years (and I can't thank her enough), that I have been able to climb out of "my prison", so to speak. I was delving into what unconditional love truly is and working on where my balancing lines and personal boundary lines were needing to be adjusted. And I was spending a lot of time alone and absorbing "me" through it all…truly understanding what self-sufficiency in love really means.

I understood that this person's actions, choices and reactions, were having to do with whatever pain, anger and fear was stuck within them, creating these issues and choices from them. Someone that is THAT practiced at being manipulative and cruel and making excuses for themselves in it, did not get to that point on their own. They had "help", from someone who was abusive to them in their past. This does not take away their own responsibility for whom they have chosen to be and their behavior in it, but it does help to explain its creation.

We were both in a low place of fear and lack of self-love. It was just showing itself on the opposite sides of an ego imbalance: him leading with his ego in an attacking toxic way toward me, in both extreme defense and offense; and me, not having a strong enough ego, or sense of self in place, to move forward in a confident healthy way, either. But no matter how something like that shows itself, the problem is actually the same within; a lack of unconditional self-love.

It took me an extremely long time to come to terms with it all. I really tried, with everything in me, for so long, to talk to him about all of this; the things I was reading, the importance of self-love, the importance of internal "shadow" work; internal imbalances and their inevitable outcomes and everything I was seeing on both sides of our situation in it all. I wanted to help him while I was helping myself! But he just couldn't hear me. He would either slam me for it, referring to my words as "crazy" and "psycho-babble", or else ignore me completely.

(But yet much later, I would find that he was using some my words and my thoughts for himself in his own work and expressions…so it must not have been such "psycho-babble" then after all right?… for him to do so…just more of the same hateful, fearful and selfish behavior).

Yes, I have battled with a tremendous amount of pain, disgust, rage and loathing toward him for everything he has done toward me. And therefore, also ended up having to battle my caring as well, because of the toxic circumstances…(in other words, caring never helped or mattered in a situation with someone that is incapable of truly caring, or being caring and real, in return. Their negative ego was clearly running the show).

But I had a bit of happiness and peace of mind at least, knowing that, within myself, I had really put in effort to do the work on myself with everything. That I had gone within and really understood where my side of things had been creating problems, but also had stood up for myself with what I knew was not my issue and therefore not my responsibility. I had owned my stuff to them plenty, even if they couldn't own theirs. And I had consistently worked to control my emotions when speaking or writing to them enough, so that I could approach them from a place of equality, even if they could not. I was grateful to myself for this. I knew that matching hateful tactics with hateful tactics, would do nothing for anybody.

I struggled with forgiveness for a very long time. I was having to work to forgive myself for the continuous struggle I have had in my life, in not being there for myself but also work to try to forgive them (and others) for their cruel behavior toward me. Forgiveness can be so incredibly painful and difficult. But what can help, is to remember that to successfully forgive someone else for cruelty toward you is not to excuse their behavior in any way. It is to be very clear within yourself on the details between what is theirs and what is yours and to release yourself from pain that you never deserved to have to feel.

The whole experience really felt like a death though. In fact, I DID go through the stages of grief like a death when trying to work through everything that had happened from both sides. Because even if just looking at it from human being to human being, bringing nothing of my pull or deep attraction to him into it, I truly cared and wanted things to be better. But it was never allowed to happen. Being able to see all of the problems from all sides but not able to lead it all to a place of a healing solution, felt like a deep loss to me.

It is a lot of why I kept emailing them though. Even if they would just selfishly use it for themselves and twist the truth in it, like everything else…I knew they couldn't and wouldn't hear me now…but in writing, they have the ability to refer back to it. And I was hoping that someday, when going back over my words, it might all finally click into place, how much I really was coming from a place of caring, but that I absolutely could not and would not put up with being treated so horribly. I was just trying to find the place of equality, that I had always deserved and had always been willing to give them, if they could ever go there. I don't care about competition and I have never come from a place of needing to be "better than", because I know it doesn't really exist. I just wanted to be able to be "me" and they could be "them", but it had to be sitting in a place of honesty, respect and healthy equality. The toxicity would have to end.

But yes, I also knew that I could not continue in such a one-sided, futile situation with someone who could not even treat me with decency and with the same openness that he had always been selfishly demanding of me. He would attack me and then play the victim. His illusions, fears and aggressive walls were so high, there was never going to be any penetration of them.

And all I can say now is, if he ever truly felt tortured by what had happened, as he acted like he has…saddened and like he had been "attacked" by me…then he is an example of someone stuck in the deepest forms of avoidance and self-delusion I have ever seen. He is someone that seriously needs to stop and go within. You can say accurately that being stuck in such a toxic situation with someone, that was succeeding in tearing me down, can be called self-abuse to a degree, yes. That nobody can hurt you, unless you technically let them. But it still doesn't take away his responsibility in the fact that he WAS attacking me, in order to avoid his own issues, and to try to feed his negative ego, at my expense.

And it is just as true then, that to be an abuser toward another person, is to abuse yourself. With every action you deliberately take to harm another person and to try to make them feel "less than", use them, or try to control them, you are truly abusing yourself too. They are not separate. A person who attacks people for their negative ego is a person that is creating their own hell and dragging other people down with them, (if the target of the attack is unable to defend themselves from it, like I was). So I take responsibility for my part in it but I refuse to take responsibility for theirs!

If I had been in a better, more balanced place, things would have happened very differently and I would not have ended up in such a toxic and painful situation.

I admit too though, I still have not completely gotten over it. I still mourn this situation and this person; that it could never be dealt with in a mutual healing way…just even as human being to human being. So the best I have been able to do, is to come to a type of acceptance of it…because I cannot make someone see something they don't want to see, or do something they don't want to do. And I cannot and will not be treated like that. Anybody who treats me in these ways cannot be in my life. And if they can't see why it should change for either of us, or care about changing it, then it just has to stay how it is.

******

The third situation ended up overlapping a large part of both the 1st and 2nd experiences, so again, it was a build. This man came around during the worst of everything I had been going through. And at first, they came out of nowhere and seemed like they were truly going to be a wonderful friend. And their extended group of friends looked like they would end up being great friends as well. I got extremely close with him over a long period of time. He didn't live near me, so we would talk a lot over the phone and arrange a few times in the year that we could all get together.

They all seemed like a breath of fresh air to me. And he seemed to be the opposite of what I was used to, generally speaking (with the exception of a couple of people); a friend that would go out of their way for me. A friend that understood me and I understood them. We were able to be there for each other through difficult times and they didn't seem to judge me in any of it. I eventually ended up confiding in them with all of the hell I had been going through with the previous two people, but also sharing some other situations with them regarding people I had come across or had been dealing with, around that same time-frame.

Some were situations where guys were interested in me but I wasn't interested in return...or else if I was in any bit of a way, I just needed to change the speed of things, or change the approach the other person was taking with me. But in either case, once I voiced how I felt to them, trying very hard to be as sincere and caring as I could with it, they would still come at me with a bunch of criticism and slander, like I was a lesser person and wasn't worth anything. It was obvious that these people's egos had gotten hurt and felt rejected. And instead of handling it in a nice or respectful way, had to attack me to make themselves feel better. You would think I would have been used to that type of behavior by that point...and in some ways, was starting to be; in the sense that I was starting to feel myself slowly pulling away from those situations in emotional ways, and knowing that I didn't deserve any of it. It wasn't affecting me quite as deeply as it used to, but it was still hurting me.

But I also had confided in him about a long time friend of mine that I finally had made the painful decision to let go of. It was a situation where, I had really been there for this person through so much pain and difficulty in their life. Many years of it. And I always put out effort for her. But once I hit rock bottom during the period of leaving my ex and struggling through the other two people that I have mentioned, along with dealing with other life stresses and really needed a friend, she could only think about herself. It became a type of situation where they were saying that my difficulty was basically "bringing them down". It was a tremendously selfish slap in the face, because I never treated them like that, when they were going through difficult times. And they proved very clearly that they did not value all of the time and caring I had given them over the years. They could not be an equal friend to me. So I ended that friendship. I deserved better and knew it. I was done...

Over time, this 3rd person ended up confiding to me the issues in his life as well. He had grown up in an abusive home. He had also been abusive to others. This was the first time I had had someone confide to me in a lot of the selfish and cruel things they had done to people, quite like he had. And I just listened. But of course, this person talked about it with remorse and like it was all what they "used to be like".

During the breakdown that I had had, they seemed to really be there for me through it. But it eventually started to change.

They said that they loved me for me and just wanted me to be happy. But eventually, because I wasn't happy and was still trying to get over everything that happened, to work through it all and was still reading and deeply thinking about it all, they started to get upset with me because I wasn't "letting myself move on", according to them, and wasn't just "being happy". (But also because I wasn't just letting it all go and focusing my attention on them and the things they wanted me to focus on).

But also too, because there was a very key conversation that occurred with them one night where we had been talking about the emails between the previous person and I. We had been talking about abusive behaviors and tactics. And he had been getting short with me for a while up to that point, whenever we would talk about the previous guy. And he finally admitted it was because it was difficult for him to talk about, because looking at those types of tactics and behaviors is similar to what he does, and he didn't want to admit to himself that he was truly "abusive". I couldn't understand that fully, considering that he had already talked about himself to me in depth and had told me some very horrible things that he had done to people. What else would that be, if not abuse?! It was obvious that he was still in denial of it all fully and had continued to make excuses for himself in it. So I replied simply that it was definitely abuse but if he was unsure about it, then maybe he should read up on

56

it all some more, to help for more information.

But yes, throughout everything, we had become close friends and he said that he cared for me and truly enjoyed my company. He said that he deeply appreciated that I was someone that he could talk to about anything. He appreciated my strength and caring, even in the face of some of the deep rage and anger I was dealing with. He appreciated my ability to look at all sides of things. He appreciated that I was there for him. And on and on with the compliments…

But like I said, as time wore on, he started saying that my inability to heal was my own fault. That I was someone who was just wallowing and needed to snap out of it. That I wasn't doing anything active and forward moving to help myself.

I understood what he was saying only to a certain degree, but in my mind, I WAS doing something very active! All of the internal work I was doing was something that was incredibly necessary. I knew I was needing to gain a stronger foundation for myself. I knew that people were too easily dumping on me with their ego-based issues and that I was needing to find the balance, the love and the strength within myself to get to a point where that type of thing could no longer have an effect on me. I needed to get to the point where I was walking through the world, in as much balance as possible, no matter what was happening in my life or how someone behaves toward me. I knew that with balanced inner energy, my outer life would then start to change for the better, in all ways.

Again, I was deeply reading and really trying to figure out how I felt about things, what I believed, and what was my complete truth in dark and in light. I was seeing the effects of the weight I had been carrying around all of my life and how it was holding me back and creating problems for myself. I was seeing my imbalances, but also seeing the imbalances of the people I was dealing with.

And I was looking at anything that was an emotional trigger for myself, no matter how mundane or how huge, and really making sure I understood where it is coming from and why, and then deciding how I felt about it and how I wanted to approach the situation. I was taking my power back, one small step at a time! That was NOT something small and mundane and definitely not something that could ever be labeled "wallowing"!

And in fact, I could see that this type of inner work was something he clearly avoided and seriously needed to do for himself, in a MAJOR way!!!

But yes, I did not have balance yet to my life. I was not going out and trying to make new friends…the deep disappoints from the past and the fear for more of the same, was still there. I was having some successes with outside artistic projects, but still struggling in a lot of ways with fear with that, as well. I was in a job that I did not enjoy and not exactly living in a place that was comfortable either. And I still could not get myself to even think about approaching trying to date someone...I was still hung up on everything that happened. I was at a point where I would rather be alone, then to ever have one more negative situation happen again.

So yes, I understood that they just wanted me to be happy. They just wanted me to be in a happy state that I could exist with them in. But what do you do if you just aren't fully there yet?!

I was really trying. And I felt like I was really making headway within myself. I was feeling better about myself over time. I was speaking up for myself much more. I was trying to focus on the positive things in my life. I was finding a balance for myself...it was slow, but it was happening.

But they started to really take all of it into themselves, to the point where, if I didn't have the "right" mood or approach to something, according to them and what they wanted, they would start to come down on me for it. This was the beginning of the end for us.

I would stand up for myself and he only started to get more and more hyper-critical and nasty with me over time; to the point where everything that had been said to be a positive about me, was now being painted as a negative. He twisted everything around on me. One example being, that where they had said in the past that they appreciated that I was someone who could really be there for someone, no matter how low of a state they were in, and really be able to just listen to them. It was now being changed to be considered a lowly quality and weak, because he was trying to say that I am someone who encourages a wallowing state by that behavior and I don't push the person to change. (A convenient change of mind, since he was feeling better about things in his own life now and wasn't needing me to be there in that particular way for him anymore). But it also showed me how he will use and twist absolutely anything in order to "win" and be considered "better than". But I knew it was complete crap, because I don't need, want, or desire to dictate to someone. It isn't for me to dictate to anyone. I can make suggestions, I can be there for a person, I can listen, but I will not dictate. That isn't a weakness, that is a strength! And that is called actually being a friend. I cannot completely help anyone out of anything, just like nobody can completely help me out of anything, (nor do I expect them to). People have to help themselves. But other people can support. It was obvious to me that this person was only thinking about themselves.

Who I was, and everything that was happening in my life was starting to be attacked, because they could only think about how it affected THEM and how they demanded I should be. And because I wasn't handling things in the ways that they would handle things, or what was comfortable for them, it was automatically deemed "less-than", weak, lowly, and unworthy.

But you can look at anybody on this planet and see things that need to change, be improved on, etc. Nobody is immune or an exception to that. So for them to be attacking me in those ways was deeply hurtful and completely unacceptable, because I could look at them and pick out PLENTY of things they needed to improve on and change...but I am not someone that needs to pull that kind of crap with people. But it is a situation where, if someone crosses the line with me and starts attacking me, then yes, I can look at it all from both sides and have some ownership and speak about it, but I will NOT be made "low"...which means they will get a very large "mirror" held up for them in return, for their choice in attack, with a very large magnifying glass tuned into their "stuff". If there is no equality, then there is no point...especially considering where I have been coming from in my life. I will not be used for people anymore, or have someone treat me with entitlement.

The more we talked, the more we only ever ended up fighting, because they were demanding that I do, be, think and feel what they wanted, how they wanted it, when they wanted it. And if I didn't, I was deemed weak, lowly, wrong and on and on.

It eventually turned into an all out berating from them: where I was painted to be over-sensitive, over-thinking, weak, negative, unattractive and selfish. They said that I was "going to be alone" and said it in a way that was as much of a judgment, as it was a threat. They said that "no man would ever want me". And the lowest of the low, was that they started acting just like the previous person had with me and even started using their words and their tactics to attack me with, because they knew I was still trying to heal from it all. They said that that person was right to do everything that they had done. That I deserved it all. That I was actually the person that was the entire problem. And not only in this person's case, but in every single situation I had ever been in. That I was a horrible, crazy and sick person. It was ALL always me!

It all makes me think of when they told me that they were once taught by an "anger-management" class that they should "avoid anybody who is an emotional trigger". To me, that is the most ridiculous advice I have ever heard!... and actually extremely detrimental to the client. That is giving this person with abusive angry tendencies, yet one more EXCUSE they can give themselves to dump blame, judgment and criticism onto another person, in order to avoid themselves entirely. That doesn't solve anything!!! These people NEED to address the real issues within themselves, take their individual power back, stop pointing fingers and attacking people, and take responsibility for what is truly creating these triggered behaviors within themselves. Truly face it and take control of themselves. And now, yes, this person was trying to say that I was the unhealthy person that was CAUSING him suffering. But just by taking that stance, he was being a massive hypocrite. If he is going to say that my upset was my fault, then I can just as easily say that his upset was his fault! But I wasn't attacking him though. HE was attacking me. So it was all absolutely ridiculous. But just like the people before him, when I would try to talk to them about everything, I WAS owning my sides of things, addressing things, working with everything and being equality driven but I was definitely standing up for myself too, this person could only selfishly attack. So I was just so incredibly hurt and completely fed up.

Unfortunately there were times too, when my anger and pain would get the better of me and I raised my voice and swore. This person harped on that like no tomorrow!....used it for themselves and called me "abusive and out of control". It was just, yet another, bullying tactic. Yes, raising your voice and swearing isn't going to help anything, but this person was doing FAR WORSE and knew it. All they cared about was using anything they could grab onto to "win" and make me wrong. No empathy or caring was in existence at all. Narcissistic and sociopathic behavior through and through.

After everything I had been through, with them having seen me and experienced me at the lowest, most painful place I had ever been in, in my life, to have them USE it all for themselves as a weapon...to have them turn on me in such a completely sadistic way, did succeed in crushing me for a while. I sent them one hell of a long email expressing all kinds of truths from all sides. They had had a chance to finally address themselves in their own abusive tendencies, once and for all, to STOP their abusive cycle. But once again, they chose to attack and run.

Having someone judge you in how long it takes you to heal from a trauma is like judging someone and criticizing them for how long it takes someone to recover from the death of a loved one. I see them as extremely similar in how ridiculous they are. Grief and healing are deeply personal and individual things that NOBODY has a right to judge or put a stipulation on. And if they do, then they are just selfishly thinking about themselves – their own wants, how your situation affects them, their needs, desires and where they "demand" that you should "be" for them, so they don't have to confront and deal with themselves.

I remember that he used to say to me that the abuse he suffered from his family only made him stronger. That they did him a "favor" and served to "toughen him up." And my response to that is that abusive people only destroy. Period. If any strengthening comes out of the situation, the credit does not go to the abuser. It goes to the "target" of the abuse. But ONLY if the target can say that they have come out of it stronger in the sense that they have come out of it still able to be a loving, equality-driven person, despite the abuse. If the target chooses to let themselves become the abuser, then they are choosing to be just as much of an empty, hate-filled soul as the abuser. It becomes a behavior of selfishness and self-entitlement then...like, "I was hurt in my past, so I am going to destroy anybody and everybody who ever goes against me in some way, regardless of the true overall circumstances...and I will try to destroy anybody who points out my faults in reasoning, things that need to be improved or changed, weaknesses, etc." And that is supposed to be powerful?!

But what became very different about this incident, compared to the rest, was that I was down for a much shorter amount of time. I was extremely devastated, hurt and angry, yes. But it did not destroy me for such a long period of time as before…because I could REALLY see the truth. With having already "been there, done that", with so much abusive crap from people before and so much imbalance from others and myself, I knew I wasn't seeing anything incorrectly. And I knew I wasn't being "selfish", like they were trying to say I was for themselves. I knew I was really trying to go within and face everything within myself to find inner balance, so that my outer life could start to reflect that balance too. I was standing up for myself! And I had REALLY tried to have a true conversation with them about it all…not a fight.

But habitually outwardly abusive people will use and say anything to "win". There is no equality, because in order for there to be in any equality, they would have to address their own issues, faults, fears and weaknesses with complete honesty. But the negative side of their ego won't let them. They are in a constant state of childish, ego-feeding tantrum, with the viciousness of an adult mind. It is attack based in fear. Everything is about competition with them. They have to be "better than" and the "winner", when it is all completely ridiculous and does nothing for them; it's not real.

I know what that feeling is like to have so much rage at the unjust and ridiculous amount of abuse I have suffered at the hands of hate-filled people…as well as rage at myself for not being there for myself. I know what it is like to be pushed to the tipping point with it all and have to pull yourself back down to a more balanced thought process. And even with intellectually knowing that another person's behavior is not my issue, to still have to deal with the emotional pain and torment of it all…trying to come to terms with all of it and to heal. It is a deep pain and loss I was feeling at the realization that these people are too blinded by needing to be "right" or "better than", to ever be able to stand up and take their power back. They cannot be in my life. As long as they stay in that place, they absolutely cannot be. They don't care enough about themselves, or about me, to be better people. So I was feeling the loss of them.

It can make you overreact then, when you feel even the list bit pushed at, talked down to, or attacked by someone. It can make you feel like being alone is just flat out safer and the best possible choice for yourself. You can feel hyper-on-guard, constantly ready in fight-or-flight for yourself…but the difference between me and them, is that when I fight, I fight for BALANCE for BOTH sides. The reason being, I know all too well, that if you're not careful, you can become abusive yourself, just like they have! That is how the "abuse-disease" spreads. I have had enough rage in me to go there. But I know that abusers think they are protecting themselves, or even gaining something over someone else, to attack or manipulate someone…but it is wrong. It is only an illusion of the negative, needy side of the ego and a result of the poisonous pain within them that they are not facing and dealing with, (or just cannot control), that is telling them that.

If an outwardly abusive person cannot stop and really face everything that is happening within themselves and take control of their emotions, the deeper negative truths within themselves, have self ownership, etc., they will never heal and they will never change. And they will continue to keep projecting onto others, using people to feed their egos; bullying people and attacking others for themselves.

Just like on the opposite spectrum that I was in. If an inwardly abusive person does not face themselves and doesn't question and fight against all of the fear-based, unworthy feelings they can tend to have toward themselves, that holds them back in life and makes them targets… and doesn't start to stand up and push back for themselves when needed, embrace themselves and their unique personal power, then they won't be able to change either, and they will keep finding themselves being torn down, both by themselves and others.

Like I had mentioned briefly earlier, this person had grown up in abuse. They had been in a parenting situation that was repeatedly verbally and emotionally abusive; doing and saying horrible things to them, along the lines that they were ugly/over-weight, worthless, stupid, not good enough, that they needed to be the best or they were nothing, and on and on. And they have now grown up. And they have turned into that abusive adult in so many ways.

They are constantly judgmental and critical. They talk a lot of crap about people behind their backs. Nobody is safe. They will claim they are caring for someone and yet treat them with disrespect and tear them down. They try to excuse it away by saying that they are giving "tough love" and that this is actually helping the other person. They will also use the excuse that they are getting angry at you and saying the things they are saying because they supposedly, "care SO much." This is someone who is still stuck in all of the negative manipulation that was drilled into their head. "You have to be the best". "No weaknesses allowed." In other words: 'Any weaknesses will be exploited, used against you and shoved down your throat. Any issue I see with you will be judged and punished. And YOUR inability to ever be perfect, will be something that I will take as a personal assault. I will tear you down with every improvement you need to make. I won't care where you are at with anything, or if there is any validity to the reasons why something is slowing you down. I won't care how much effort or progress you have already shown. I will deliberately push away your considerable amount of strengths, pluses and positive attributes and instead, slam you down for anything negative I see. I will exploit you for my ego to feel better about myself. I will even create some negativity, when it suits me to punish you, until you comply and are what I want you to be.

You will do, be, think and feel what I want, when I want, how I want. And if you fight back, by making me think about any of the weaknesses, fears, needed improvements, faults, anything that I have within myself, (because those things are absolutely NOT ALLOWED), then I will truly attempt to attack, slander and destroy you for myself. I will shun you completely and make you something ugly and worthless for myself and to others, so that they shun you too.'

That is how they operate. And that is definitely how I have been treated by these people (and also in some ways, insidiously, treated toward myself). And the more you stand up for yourself with them, the more they project onto you and twist the truth of you, to make you something ugly, horrible and lowly for themselves, rather than dealing with themselves.

This is why, over time, you can start to see that the people they keep around them are only the people they can manipulate and control. They are abusive to them too but these people don't ever entirely push back about it, because if they did, they would be attacked and shunned completely. It will always be made to be the other person's issues, weaknesses, faults, etc. And the people that stay around the abuser and let them continue in this way, get their "rewards" for staying around them and playing the game, by getting their egos fed too, off of the slammings that the abusive person gives to others…in other words, stroking their egos enough, playing on what they know these people's weaknesses and needs are, so that they stay around them, like some kind of reward. The abuser doesn't even fully respect them…but that doesn't matter. As long as they can continue in their ego-feeding games, that is all that matters to them.

I don't know if I believe that there is pure "evil" in existence within people in this world. If there is, then it is a very low percentage overall. Because I believe that most people who fall into a stereotypical "evil" category, are only there because they are too lost in hate, the need to fight/attack, toxicity, self-righteousness, selfishness, coldness, competition, self-loathing and fear, to be able to see any other truths, or any other ways of being. They do not know how to truly love themselves, so they are fearful and hateful people. They are not evil at their cores. They are just as deserving of unconditional love as the next soul. But they keep choosing behaviors that destroy love, happiness and true fulfillment from coming into their lives, or from being capable of giving it to others. They are blind because they don't understand how, or see how, they can ever truly love themselves, or be deserving of love. And with people like this, they will always cause strife, destruction, pain and separation.

Habitually outwardly abusive people are not egoically "feeding" themselves anything positive, by their behavior. That is what they seem to be completely blind to understanding. They "think" they are giving themselves a gift. They believe they are proving themselves "better than", "above", a "winner" in competition, "righteous" and on and on. But in reality, every single time a person chooses to be selfish, unjust, cold, or cruel to another person, they are actually being abusive to themselves...not just to the other person. They aren't actually gaining anything real or positive. It is an illusion of grandeur based on fear, and a lack of self love. They are pulling themselves down with their negative choices, habits and thought structures that are not coming from a place of love, neither toward the other person, or themselves. They don't see that there is actually NO separation between the two. It is an 'I am another you and you are another me', reality. There is no division from that spiritual truth. So when you choose to *"do unto others as you would have them do unto you"*, you are actually choosing a loving, equality driven path. Anything less, will have repercussions upon yourself. And I am not talking about Karma, necessarily. I am just talking very plainly about the energetic and spiritual consequences of your choices. If you lead with negative energy and negative intentions, negativity will come back to you. If you lead with positive energy and positive intentions, positivity will come back to you. This is truth. And it always shows itself in one form or another. So if you want loving, equality-driven, honest people in your life, then start by BEING that type of person. And if you are truly that type of person but someone comes into your life that cannot match your energy in that respect, then they will be removed...either by your own choices, or theirs...because the mismatch of intentions, caring and respect, will be too obvious to

71

ignore and the relationship, or situation, will inevitably crumble.

It's ironic that they can deem someone else so incredibly low, but yet they can't seem to see the deep hypocrisy in their own behavior. Their behavior, actions and reactions are low, negative, weak, toxic, selfish, hateful and fearful. But yet, somehow magically, it is always the other person's problem.

It reminds me of a few great quotes:

1) A Biblical Quote - simplified: *'Correct a fool and they will hate you; Correct a wise man and they will appreciate you.'*

2) *"Sordid selfishness doth contract and narrow our benevolence, and cause us, like serpents, to infold ourselves within ourselves, and to turn out our stings to the entire world besides."* ~ Sir Walter Scott

3) *"The difference between my darkness and your darkness is that I can look at my own badness in the face and accept its existence, while you are busy covering your mirror with a white linen sheet. The difference between my sins and your sins is that when I sin, I know I'm sinning, while you have actually fallen prey to your own fabricated illusions. I am a siren; a mermaid; I know that I am*

beautiful while basking on the ocean's waves and I know that I can eat flesh and bones at the bottom of the sea. You are a white witch, a wizard; your spells are manipulations and your cauldron from hell, yet you wrap yourself in white and wear a silver wig." ~ C. JoyBell C.

So, why was I "low"? Because I was trying to get out of a difficult place? Because I can actually admit when I'm wrong and that something needs to improve? Because I can admit fear? … To me, that will always be a strength, not a weakness.

For myself, it has almost been like I have been living my entire life as two people. And these people can see all of the psychological pieces of myself, so to speak: (male, female, father, mother, sister, brother, inner child, inner metaphoric animals, etc.) and which side they had fallen on. One side, being the side that could see so clearly into my strengths, talents, positivity and the immense capacity for love and compassion that I have available to myself and to others. This side could take a compliment and have gratitude for it being seen as truth. While the other side could only see my faults, weaknesses, and any reasons it could throw out there, (in truth or not), why I didn't deserve love and was unworthy, and would therefore question everything that was said to me.

The majority of the split has come together to be much more of a cohesive "family". I have proven so much to myself that is positive and immensely strong throughout all of this difficulty. I have gone through abuse and still fought like hell to remain someone who is equality driven and loving; not fearful and hateful. I have proven that even in the face of abuse, extreme selfishness and aggression from others, I can stand up for myself and really take the time to try and get my message across to the other person, as well as to take in their side, so that my communication can be one of movement toward healing. Whether they can do anything about it on their end, is another story, and not something I can put on myself. But what matters is that I tried and I truly cared...about myself and about them, enough to do it.

But I know I still have some work to do. My sensitivity has always been acute. I am an empath that has been struggling for stronger energy protection. And I still have times of "bracing" myself, as well as difficulty with anger. But it is much improved.

The key though, that I have to keep reminding myself, is that it isn't about trying to stop the feeling of "bracing" myself necessarily. Because let's face it, these things will happen again in various ways and percentages at times in my life. So, it is actually more about keeping myself firmly in as much of a place of balanced love for myself and for others as I can, so that if someone does do anything unjust and deliberately cruel toward me, I am not letting it dump onto me or am taking it upon myself...that I keep their responses, their issues and their questionable intentions, fully theirs. Once there, that feeling of "bracing" will just fall away naturally.

The affects of abuse can make the world a very dark place; stuck in fear. For the outwardly abusive, it becomes a fear based world leading to constant competition, negative judgment, and cruelty. These people don't speak their true feelings, don't admit their fears, can't admit when they are wrong and can't be vulnerable and open, and play emotional and mental games, because they are trying to control everything and because they refuse to face themselves. And the "power" they gain in tearing others down isn't real. REAL power has always been and always will be LOVE. But with their habitual behavior, they are stuck in an offensive and defensive loop that will destroy love, truth and equality.

For the inwardly abusive, it becomes a fear based world leading to putting others before yourself and not speaking your heart and mind enough for fear of being attacked, put down, or negatively misunderstood. They don't want competition and spite. They want things to be neutral and caring, but often go out of their way to create that environment for the other person, but not enough for themselves. They can get stuck in a self-defeating loop that will destroy love, truth in the belief in themselves and in the ability to enforce equality for themselves.

Do you see the similarities yet? Because I definitely did. And have been working with them now for a long time.

I feel like the side of the spectrum that I have been on might have the slightly lesser mountain to climb though, in order to get back to balance, because getting back to balance involves going deep within and being very thorough about what needs to change and what needs to be strengthened. Since the inwardly abusive side is already used to combing themselves over in this way (and usually overly so), it is easier for them to see truths, own them and move forward.

However, the habitually outwardly abusive spectrum has the equivalent of their own personal Mt. Everest to climb, because this side has spent their entire lives repeatedly running from the darker truths and intentions within themselves and dumping and projecting them onto others. With someone like that, their fear and a very necessary type of "negative ego-death" will need to happen. But it won't happen, unless they realize how much of an offensive and defensive destructive self-labeled "crutch" their behavior has been and how much of an actual detriment it is for them to continue in it. This is why so many of them that sit in this extreme area on the spectrum, rarely do anything about any of it. They continue running and making excuses for themselves, they never heal and continue to keep using and abusing people for themselves. And deliberately surround themselves with people who will let them continue in it.

For me, I could look at these people for EVERYTHING that they were, good and bad. And the good was considerably good! So much so, that it made me physically, mentally, emotionally and spiritually ill to go through these incredibly painful experiences with them. But the majority of my pain was not in the considerable amount of anger and trauma I experienced in being treated so horribly…it was in the ability to see exactly what the problems were, know how to fix them, but yet know that I cannot make anybody see reality if they refuse to see it. I cannot make anybody want to be a healthier, better person. I cannot make somebody love themselves if they can't see why they should. I cannot make somebody see what an absolute waste of time, waste of their precious lives, and of their precious true core selves, this choice in illusionary and destructive behavior is. I cannot make them see that deep down, they are deserving of love, just like everybody on this planet is deserving of love. I cannot make them see that if they would only make the choice to let love, self-honesty, self-ownership and some self-control into the picture, then they would be able to start to take their power back, instead of living their lives in a constant state of tantrum, attack and negative reaction. And I could understand this, because I had been coming out of it, in my own ways toward myself, with my own imbalances.

Any other choice than love, is a waste and an abuse of the very spirit! Loving yourself into a healed, balanced state is the only remedy for this but you have to face yourself to do it….no matter where your imbalances lie.

I could see it and that was EXACTLY what I was doing!

It has made me want to shake them awake! Scream! Cry! Yell from the rooftops! Do anything I can, to get them to see the wonderful world and life this could be, if they would only truly go through the steps and make the effort to face themselves, deal with themselves, their fears and their inner demons; have self-ownership and CHOOSE better!!! Choose equality. Choose LOVE. That it isn't up to everybody else to make things ok for them, do their bidding, take their abuse, etc. Nobody exists for another person. They have to stand up and BE what they want to create and to receive!

We all do.

Live a mindful life that really pays attention, so that you can and do, put your best feet forward. You can't do that if you are constantly ignoring the darker sides of yourself that need to be addressed, worked with and gained some control over, so you can then learn how to love them. Pushing them away, will only make them show themselves in more and more destructive ways, over time.

And I am being very honest with you all, when I say that I have genuine love, in general, for all of the people who have been in my life, in both good and in bad. And even though some of these people were incredibly cruel, ugly and horrible to me, I have truly cared and have only wanted to help them out of this circular poisonous cycle…in the same ways that I have taken so much time, energy and care in removing myself from any of my own poisonous cycles that have been wreaking havoc and causing painful blockages in my own life. I can see these things all so clearly, but also know it takes time, effort and repetition to clear them out.

I have come across a lot of people that look down their noses at self-help books, workshops, or gatherings. And to me, that only shows me a person who is being triggered into negative judgment and criticism, because they have plenty of issues within themselves that they don't want to face. People have a tendency to attack what they don't want to see within themselves. Again, this is why I say, that focusing on self-help, self-improvement and self-healing, will always be a huge show of STRENGTH in a person, never a weakness.

In the same way that being a loving person, will always be a strength, never a weakness. What the other person does has nothing to do with you. If you match another person's hate with more hate, then you are sinking yourself to their level, in an energetic sense. (Yes, I understand that it can sometimes be a very difficult thing to not get triggered by another person's "stuff"). But if you are coming from a place of love, honesty and equality, then you will always be coming from a place of strength.

Like Wayne Dyer has so accurately said, *"How someone treats you is their Karma, how you react is yours."*

No matter what you come up against in life, especially when faced with extreme cruelty and selfishness from others, find comfort in Love and Oneness. BE LOVE; Even if others cannot; KNOW that nobody can hurt you unless you let them. (That is the hardest one to learn and to truly sink into yourself, both intellectually and emotionally! I am about 70% there so far but I admit, I am still working through a lot of residual pain and anger triggers…but I'm getting there). And know that nobody can "lower" you, because there is no such thing as anybody being better than, or lower than, another. There are only better than and lower than choices, actions, reactions and behaviors. We are all equal souls, deserving of unconditional love.

But who we are as these individual human identity consciousness' in this particular time and place, is our choice, every day. You either choose healthy and equality-driven choices, with an intentional embrace in love, or you choose fearful and hateful choices, in the absence of love. It's your choice. It is nobody else's responsibility. So choose responsibly. Love yourself enough, to choose Love.

~

Chapter 3

Relationships Are Mirrors

Wayne Dyer has said, *"You don't attract what you want; you attract what you are."*

I had to think about this one for a long time. But over time, I have come to understand exactly what he means. And he is right.

Relationships of all kinds, are mirrors. They can be mirrors born out of direct similarities, or similarities in opposition. But either way, you can see into yourself very clearly, if you are caring enough about yourself and about others, to pay attention.

We also are in control of what we see and how we choose to see.

Society then, is a mirror of us all, collectively. This goes way beyond negative energy equaling more negativity and vice-versa. This is about the necessity for "shadow" work.

We all have a "shadow" side to our individual psyches. Our shadow is the repository of all of the things within us that we don't like to see or to own within ourselves, so we try to repress it, project it onto others, or deny it completely. But the Shadow side cannot be destroyed. It is a necessary part of us, just like the rest. The Shadow

81

can even be very helpful to you and to others, if you learn how to work with it, rather than reject it.

So in relationships, we are faced then with "the other". And you have to be very careful in discerning what is someone else's "stuff" and what is actually yours. You owe it to yourselves and to others, to do this type of work. That is choosing a mindful, loving existence. That is BEING Love.

It is not "out there"! It is inside of you. YOU choose what you see and what you experience, as well as how you experience it. But you will never see anything accurately, until you see yourself accurately.

The best and most truly loving gift that anybody on this planet can give themselves, and by extension then, everyone else around them, is to go deep within themselves and shine a light on the "shadow" aspects of themselves; the jealousies, fear, "better than" competitive behaviors or "less than" thoughts, over-giving behaviors, inequality, ego-driven criticism, inner or outer judgments, anger and hate, control issues, and on and on, that they can find within themselves…face them head on…and OWN them, instead of pushing it away, or trying to project it onto someone else to escape it. The more a person clears out and pays attention to themselves on a daily basis: their emotions, behaviors, actions and reactions, and checks them at the time…in order to make sure they are seeing the reality of what is truly underneath them from themselves and can make the choice to choose much more loving, compassionate and equality driven actions and reactions...the more they will be able to start releasing these negative aspects (or at the very least, having better control over them) and the love they feel toward themselves will grow. And the love and compassion they feel toward others will grow as well, simultaneously.

In this sense then, in many ways, it is the darkness within us that can open the door to the full capacity of the light we actually hold! Do not push things away! Open yourself to them and to understanding them, so that you can learn how they can be a benefit to you and to others, not a hindrance! The darkness can then become an ally and a teacher for yourself and for others. This is how you can learn to love everything that you are: both the dark and the light.

~

Chapter 4

Moving Duality into Unity

I keep seeing people with seeming fortresses around them that are fortified to the gills with weaponry for attack and all kinds of radical defensive mechanisms. They live their lives in this constant state.

But if you look at a young child, you often see an example of someone who doesn't have a fortress at all, because they have no understanding of why they would ever need one. They are completely themselves, because they know nothing else. They are open and authentic.

The challenge for all of us then, as we age, is to realize that to live in this human existence, we do need to develop a type of defensive structure for ourselves. And this structure needs to serve as a boundary for us, so that we are able to keep space and freedom for ourselves enough to be able to "BE" truly ourselves and live openly, without the influence of other people's actions, reactions, energy, etc. It serves as a defense or home-base for us. But the most important distinction that needs to be made, is that you get to choose what your structure is made of.

Is it fortified to the gills, poised in fear and attack, with the walls being built of the thickest, most impenetrable materials and fiercest weaponry you can create?

Or, what if you could picture instead, a structure made simply in love and of love, that had no need whatsoever for weaponry or extreme defensive measures? What if it were just simply the structure itself, with a drawbridge and that is it?

With this structure then, you are simply able to be "You" and if someone comes along that is trying to control you, dictate to you, manipulate, attack, etc., you can just simply draw up your bridge for yourself, energetically speaking. It doesn't necessarily mean shunning the boundary crosser, (unless you are truly needing to remove yourself) but you can still communicate with them in truths, if real communication can exist. But this is a loving space that you keep for yourself. And you can choose to open your drawbridge freely to others as well – always coming from a space of love; not fear.

You have to be able to hold your own space, in order to be your most effective higher self in this existence. So this structure becomes a type of personal energy protection. Nothing more.

My issue was that I never really had a safe structure in place for myself while growing up and I stayed that way for too long. And then when I did create a structure, it was really just a poorly built defensive one, with maybe some weak weaponry placed on it, that really didn't work well or do much. I say this somewhat laughingly but I am also very serious.

Now, I understand the difference very clearly. And I want to help others understand it as well.

It becomes about the necessity for internal balance. If you have internal balance, then you don't need anything for offense or defense. Those behaviors cancel each other out and become unnecessary.

And if we are going to focus on internal balance, then I think an extremely good place to start is on the deeper definition of internal balance.

Anita Moorjani, who I briefly mentioned earlier, has had a Near Death Experience. And as a result, she has written two wonderful books about her experience and about the importance of self-love. She has said, '*that you can measure every individual by an ego scale and an empathy scale. The ego scale – representing the person's identification with "The Self". And an empathy scale – representing the person's identification with "The Other". And in order to be in balance, or in our highest personal alignment, then we should have both scales turned up to 100%.*'

I like her definition. I understand what she is saying and I do agree with her meaning. However, I would like to change her imagery for it, just a bit.

She is right too, when she mentions in her writing that in our
society, having a strong ego has been ingrained in us to automatically
equate that with someone who is "egotistical" – or overly full of
themselves. It is defined as something negative. I agree with her that
our societal approach toward ego needs to be shifted. And in my
opinion, it is a matter then of more clearly defining what a "strong
ego" is supposed to mean.

As human beings, we need our egos to function and survive.
They are a part of our individual consciousness. However, the idea
of having your ego turned all the way up to 100%, on its own, makes
me think then, of someone who has no room for empathy; they are
completely self-serving. The same with empathy then, in reverse. So
it seems to make more sense to me that the ideal placement for both
the ego and empathy spectrums, is right in the middle, at 50%. That
way, a healthier ego emerges, that is balanced in its own light and
dark aspects and sits in a place that does not need to compete, or
separate itself from anyone. And a healthier level of empathy
emerges, that is more balanced between self and other.

We are all made up of dark & light, subconscious & conscious,
female & male energies. And in order to be balanced in general, we
would need to be able to balance those sides, or aspects of ourselves,
as well. Which means balancing give & take with others. It means
balancing passive and aggressive natures; nurturing & controlling

energies.

There is nobody in existence that does not have all of these aspects within themselves. And where there are imbalances within these aspects, they will inevitably show themselves and be mirrored on the individual's scales of ego and empathy.

So for example, if someone is abusive and controlling toward others, then they are attacking for themselves, without thinking much at all about how the other person feels. In this example then, their ego scale would be up at a much higher percentage, while their empathy percentage would be much lower. The ego and empathy scales are connected then and move interchangeably, to equal 100% combined, for each individual. So if you rated this abusive person's ego spectrum at, say, 85%...then their empathy spectrum would be at 15%. And if this same abusive person were to take the time to do some inner work on themselves and eventually start to find more balance within over time, then it would mean their empathy toward others would eventually increase in percentage, while their egocentric focus would decrease, moving both scales more toward the center balanced line.

For myself, I have had my empathy scale percentage up too high; putting others before myself and putting out too much energy toward people that did not deserve it, compared in measurement to how I was being treated. So, in order to move more toward an inner balance within myself, I have had to work on strengthening my boundaries with people, see and feel my strengths, own my talents and worth and become much more in touch with unconditional loving energy for myself, so that my ego scale could grow, lowering the empathy scale, until they both reach a percentage that is much more near a balanced center. I am definitely getting there.

Again, I understand Moorjani's 100%, parallel line, percentage scale definition. But I am changing it to an interchangeable parallel line scale, with a center balance for this discussion, because I feel like it addresses more of our natural state of dark and light qualities that we all possess. It takes working with mindful self-control, unconditional loving energy and the active embrace of our darker sides, while keeping our lighter sides in a reasonable state, to find our individual internal balance.

~

Chapter 5

Your Personal Rating Scales

If you were to rate yourself on the scales of ego and empathy right now, where would you be?

Whether the answer is difficult or easy for you to say at this time or not, I have put together some questions for you to think about, that might either make it easier to come to a conclusion, or else make you think much more deeply about your initial answer.

Some questions for thought:

How negative is your self-talk? Pay attention to your thoughts for a few days straight, to see how positive or negative you are toward yourself, others, your environment, situations and ideas.

How often can you admit you're wrong about something to yourself, let alone outwardly to others? And how often can you truly apologize?

How often do you talk badly about others? And how often can you say, without doubt or question, that whatever you are saying about them is justified, completely true and absolute? And similarly, what about venting? When you are venting, do you have the ability to vent while still talking about all sides of an issue, even if there are pieces that go against yourself? Or does venting automatically equal bashing someone or something else?

How often can you tell that someone is uncomfortable with, or even hurting from, something you're doing but you continue to do it anyway? What do you tell yourself at these times?

How often do you make excuses for your own flaws, weaknesses and mistakes but yet slam others for theirs? Or the reverse: How often do you make excuses for others flaws, weaknesses and mistakes but yet slam yourself for yours? And if you are a mix of both…what are your percentages?

Are you someone who can remove yourself, your needs and your judgments, when someone else is down and struggling with a long time problem? Can you really sit and listen and just be there for them, without feeling negatively toward them and needing to tell them what they "need" or "should" be doing? Are you truly able to see things from their point of view? Do you try to put yourself in their shoes? Or do you approach people from how you would handle their situation and give your judgments and opinions from there?

How often do you compare yourself to others? And how often do you see yourself as better than or less than others?

How often do you feel compelled to compete with others and/or prove yourself in some way to others? And when you compete, what is your level of need within yourself to win?

How often do you do something for someone and can say that you are doing it all truly for them? Or how often are you doing things for others - but actually doing it to be seen a certain way by them; or wanting to be liked; to feel needed; or be viewed as more capable than others; wanting to get the person to trust you; wanting the person to feel "obligated" to you in some way; or to get the person into a certain "place or mindset" for you in some way; or doing something for them so that they will do something for you?

Would you say that you need others in your life, or do you simply choose people to be in your life?

How often does fear underline your choices, actions and reactions? How often does anger underline your choices? How often does needing and wanting to control other people or situations for yourself, underline your choices?

What are your intentions toward people, on average?

How comfortable are you alone? Do you feel comfortable eating alone at a restaurant? Or taking a vacation alone? How often do you spend alone time with activities that just "fill the time" (like with TV, Movies, Social Media, etc.), versus truly spending time with yourself?

How dependant on outside factors or other people are you, in order to feel peaceful, happy, accepted and content?

How often do you stop yourself from being vulnerable and showing it?

How often do you stop yourself from trying new things?

How often do you feel that others are trying to do something negative toward you, or take something from you? And if you ever have any clear evidence or illumination of any of it, how often are you right or wrong?

If you had a son or daughter and they were going to date someone who was just like you, how comfortable would you be with that? Why, or why not?

What do you value? How much of your life and your behaviors live up to those values? How much does the behavior of the people around you measure up to those values?
Or in other words: What are you ultimately wanting in the people around you? Then look at yourself and ask yourself if you match everything that you are wanting.

Do you feel like there is enough abundance to go around for everyone in this lifetime? Or do you live by an, "it's everybody for themselves" mentality?

How often do you feel peaceful? How often are you in a state of gratitude? How often do you acknowledge the beauty that exists, not just around you but that exists in this world? Do you spend time with animals and can see their unconditionally loving, open and nurturing qualities? Do you spend time in nature and can appreciate the magnificence and beauty of it?

How often do you pay attention to your triggers, actions and reactions to things? Do you think about their causes? How often do you pay attention to other people's triggers, actions and reactions and their possible causes?

Do you see and treat people as equals? Do you equate seeing a person's flaws, weaknesses and mistakes as something disgusting and low? What about how you see your own? When you judge another person, how often are you able to ask yourself, where, when and how you may have done, or are currently doing, the exact same things that you are criticizing in them?

What are your percentages of give and take with others?

How often do you push away your instincts for change? How comfortable are you with change?

Are you real about your feelings to yourself and to others? And if not, why not? Do you look within, or do you always look outside of yourself for blame and for the reasons as to why you hold back?

Do you feel obligated to anybody? If so, why?

How has situations from your past created who you are today? Are you holding grudges or fears? What behaviors are you prone to and why?

Are you proud of yourself and who you are?

What are your strengths and weaknesses, successes and fears, flaws and mistakes? How do you feel to be looking at them? Is this exercise hard to do? If you were to list everything, how balanced in length, or lopsided, would the list be?

I know. These are a lot of questions to think about. But that is the point. Love yourself enough to take the time to really be able to answer all of the ins and outs of these questions deeply and thoroughly. You will be giving yourself a gift by doing so, as well as other people who come into contact with you.

You're not going to solve or resolve everything at once, of course, just like that. And your personal percentage ratings will tend to yo-yo a bit, before you are able to find a center. It takes a lot of deep contemplation and time, mixed with really practicing to "re-program" yourself into where you are wanting to be and then actively moving toward it. But you can't work on something if you are unable or unwilling to see a problem, (something that is no longer serving you). You have to be able to see it and own it first, before any successful change can ever happen. It is not outside of you – it is within you.

~

Chapter 6

Our Children

If I had had a class, or a mentor, as a child, that could have talked to me about the importance of self-love, about healthy ego and empathy balance, about shadow work, etc., I think it would have helped me immensely! Do NOT be fooled by anybody's age. Children have an immense capacity for deep understanding of all kinds of subjects. And being able to speak to them about these subjects; to work with them in ways that they can understand how to center themselves physically, mentally, emotionally and spiritually, could only ever have a positive impact on their development. Yes, of course, age-range specific needs would need to be in place. But I am just saying that it is possible to connect with them and to help them to grow in these ways, regardless of age.

Children go through so much! And often times, like myself when I was younger, have nowhere they can go, to really understand how to work through it all, or to even begin to know how to communicate it to someone. How can a child communicate the difficulties they are having, without environments that truly welcome the kind of equality, knowledge, caring, open communication, respect and oneness, necessary for that kind of communication...especially with more difficult subjects? I say this coming from the mindset that, even in the most loving homes, children's opinions, thoughts and emotions are often pushed aside as not being "grown up enough" to have conversations dealing with deeper subjects. But often children take in much more detail, information and emotion than people give them credit for. Sometimes much more than they even know how to express. So they just need some guidance with it.

I deeply believe that there needs to be more focus toward self-empowerment and toward cultivating deep self-love within our children. Again, this isn't an unconditional love that isn't accountable. It is a proactive, balanced love, reinforcing temperance within ego and empathy.

Children, as well as animals, are our teachers and caretakers, just as much as we can be theirs. The authenticity and simplicity of children and animals can be as eye-opening as their deep capacity for understanding, love, nurturing and equality. And even their raw emotionality and raw animal traits that could be labeled "darker" aspects, are still something that can be a great teacher. We need to ALL work together in a stronger way to help each other to grow and to evolve.

This would be guidance on the consequences of thoughts, energies and actions. It would be truly going into depth about the lighter and the darker sides of humanity, in a workable way for each age group. Truly addressing how to find balance within yourself and dealing with emotions, actions and reactions in a much more balanced way.

I have been giving great thought to how I would go about putting programs together for children of various ages, that would focus on inner balance, inner peace, equality, inner growth, self-sufficiency, oneness, etc. I would love to hear your ideas too, if you would like to share them.

Many adults are needing this type of guidance and outlet, just as much as many children, because they did not have it as children. We can help each other.

~

Chapter 7

Balance Within; So Without

What I am seeing quite a bit in society is the reflection of the individual imbalances interacting as a whole. I see a lot of beauty too. But the potential for so much more beauty and more healthy balance is there, if people can get out of their own way long enough to cultivate it. I see so many people longing for the same things: acceptance, love, respect, honesty, integrity, wholeness, peace, sanctuary, camaraderie, friendship, oneness, etc. But what people often fail to realize, is that it has always existed within them. It has never been separate from them, not for one second.

We are all spirits having a human experience…which creates the need for a balanced perspective. We are all one in a spiritual sense but we are also all our individual human ego-consciousness identities. But that spiritual core is our base. It is our home. We are never away from it. And we are all connected by it. By its very essence, it is all of those things that we all seek; it is unconditional love. We are here to find that core place within us and use it as our base, so that we can be our best individual selves and shine our individual lights of who we are, through cultivating our individual talents and strengths and sharing our authentic selves.

You have that core, unconditionally loving self within you. You just need to remember that and let all of the false walls built in fear, defense and offense that you have created for yourself, fall away, so you can embody it. Everybody is deserving of unconditional love. But they have to own it and be it, first. Where there are imbalances, they will inevitably show themselves, until they are addressed.

So many people look outside of themselves for love, worthiness, happiness and acceptance. They try to find it in other people, in actions, in fame, in financial or career success…some even try to find it in power-mongering competition and stomping down upon others, or controlling and manipulating others to feed their egos, thinking that that is filling them with something positive and proving them worthy….but it all does not actually "fill" you with anything truly full and real. And in between these "feedings" of looking outside of themselves for love, people are often trying to fill themselves in escapism and avoidance tactics as well.

People can really do themselves a huge favor by spending some time alone then, to reconnect. Truly get to know themselves. Be aware of and work through any drives that are based on neediness or avoidance. This can be a difficult process that takes time, but it is very worth it. Unplug from technology, find a space and some time alone and really go within. And if you find you are struggling with it, feeling lonely, feeling uncomfortable in any way, then do not run from it. Welcome it and really figure out its source. Sit with your feelings and just acknowledge within yourself why they are there and how necessary, or in truth, they really are. Pay attention to how you can be there for yourself more…and be in the present more.

Take the time too, to cultivate your strengths and talents. Be vigilant in growth for yourself in all capacities.

Time spent alone, is time to reconnect to your human consciousness self, as well as to your spiritual core self.

Because again, even when we are physically alone, we are never spiritually alone. Nobody NEEDS another person to be whole. We are all already whole. Yes, having a balance in social life and alone-time is ideal and healthy, but finding who you truly are is paramount for making the best of all of your experiences, whether alone or with others. We all already have everything we have ever needed or wanted, within ourselves, at our inner reach, to be whole. We just have to see it and let it all be there for ourselves.

The only thing that can fill you then, is unconditional love. You can't find it outside of yourself, if it does not exist within you. Loving yourself means working on and accepting ALL of yourself and choosing to live your life in a much more proactively balanced, loving way, toward yourself and toward others. It means taking your personal power and happiness back – no matter what someone else does or says, or what happens in your life.

Which is why, many times over, when someone is not complete within themselves, the relationships they find themselves in, often mirror their incomplete states in various ways. They can be created by the imbalances.

A relationship built on true unconditional love requires complete depth into one another. It requires complete openness and honesty to all sides. It requires an ownership of yourself and an integrity at the deepest personal level. And because of this, many relationships don't reach that level. Instead they are "conditional love", which isn't really love at all. So it becomes a relationship built in fear and all of the things that can tend to come out of fear: manipulation, dependency, competition, perceived obligation, ego battles and control.

I have been on this journey and I have seen the truths of it myself. I have always had a great capacity to be there for others, but not for myself. And in a sense, that was helping to create others not being there for me. But that compassion and understanding toward others has been great "training", so to speak, for myself, in finding the way back to loving ME. I have always understood the multiple ways that people can get off track. I have always had great compassion and understanding in that sense, but somehow not for myself. And that is something that I have changed now, over time.

I see my darkness clearly, yes, but I see my lightness just as clearly. I have a huge capacity to love. I love to get to know people and to understand them. I am an empath and a nurturer at heart. I am someone who does truly care for people and wants better for them and for myself. I am someone who loves to laugh, be spontaneous, try new things and go to new places. I am someone who has a lot of positive energy, strengths and talents that deserve to be seen. I am someone who has let other people's ugly actions, fear and hatred push me down into a "cave", that I have never deserved to be in. And that is why, now more than ever, I will ENFORCE equality, personal freedom, respect and ownership in personal integrity within any type of relationship in my life, because I know I deserve nothing less.

We are all one. So anything less than unconditional love toward ourselves and others will be hurtful universally. BE the wide open door that you are wanting to receive!

Like Osho says so succinctly in his book, "Courage": …"*To expose oneself means to expose all one's weaknesses, limitations, faults. To expose oneself ultimately means to expose one's vulnerability. Death…To expose oneself means to expose one's emptiness. Nobody can open himself like a book. Fear grips you: What will people think of me? From your very childhood you have been taught to wear masks, beautiful masks. There is no need to have a beautiful face, just a beautiful mask will do; and the mask is cheap. To transform your face is arduous. To paint your face is simple. Now suddenly to expose your real face gives you a shivering in the deepest core of your being. A trembling arises: Will people like it? Will people accept you? Will people still love you, respect you? Who knows? - because they have loved your mask, they have respected your character, they have glorified your garments. Now the fear arises: "If I suddenly become naked, are they still going to love me, respect me, appreciate me, or will they all escape away from me? They may turn their backs, I may be left alone. Hence people go on pretending. Out of fear is the pretension, out of fear arises all pseudoness. One needs to be fearless to be authentic. One of the fundamental laws of life is this: whatsoever you hide goes on growing, and whatsoever you expose, if it is wrong it disappears, evaporates in the sun, and if it is right it is nourished. The unconscious is exposed to the light and soon you gain strength because once the truth is exposed it becomes stronger and the untruth dies. And with the truth becoming stronger you become rooted, you become centered. You start becoming an individual; the personality disappears and individuality appears."*

So incredibly well said! And truly then, my question to all of you is this: For any person who attacks or shuns you, while you are being authentically you, unmasked, your individual naked self…then what does it matter?! They don't need to be in your life then. And truly, I can tell you from personal experience, that a lot of the cruel attacks and shunning I have received from certain people in my life, actually did not have everything to do with me (or my issues, etc.), the way they were trying to paint it to be…it was much more about their own

104

fear and self-loathing that created it and their inability to face themselves. Often what someone judges, criticizes and pushes away is reflecting something within themselves that they don't want to deal with or see. A trigger is just showing the person where something is needing to be healed within them.

So BE YOURSELF! UNMASK YOURSELF! FACE YOUR DEMONS, SO THAT YOUR BEST, BALANCED, UNCONDITIONALLY LOVING SELF, CAN TRULY COME FORWARD!!!! LOVE EVERYTHING THAT YOU ARE! And the people that aren't in that place with you will naturally drop away. If they treat you badly, blame you and talk horribly behind your back, let them. Who cares? They only damage themselves further, by doing so. And just know, that the people that are meant to be in your life; that can match you with the same authenticity, care for equality and inner balance; people that don't need to use you, or abuse you for their egos, will be the ones that will come into your life and will stay. So in the meantime, even if you are alone for a while...know that it is all ok. As long as you are truly coming from a place of love and working on your own balance and being the best person you can be, then that is all that matters. A balance with others will come in time. You can look at it as an invitation to become more strongly grounded within yourself and to get to know and love yourself better. Do things that challenge you, nurture you and help you to grow.

Think about how improved this world would be, if every single individual took the time out of each day to work on themselves in these ways? Doing shadow work; addressing fears, triggers, actions and reactions; spending time being more grateful and being more "present" in the now; getting out of ego and really paying attention to what others are coming across with and why; working toward a better place of mind, body and spirit health, spending more time giving back; or if they have struggled in this area, really working on enforcing boundaries with people, while still trying their best to remain equality driven in it (even if the other person can't); working on authentic communication that includes honesty and vulnerability; and on and on. If everybody started doing this type of inner work regularly, you would start to notice the effects of it very quickly. It would spread like wild fire! And that is what I am writing this for and hoping we can all start to do, collectively. The work you do individually will be reflected outward toward others. So collectively, it would be felt and seen.

We NEED more balance, love, understanding and compassion in this world! But it all starts with each of us, individually. Change what needs to change within you. Honor your true core self and live by that unconditionally loving core self; then all of the avoidance and negativity can drop away and you can choose wholeness and individual authenticity.

We are at a crossroads now. Can you feel it? There is so much chaos, corruption, hate and separation in this world…and none of it is necessary.

Each one of us has a choice in who and what we are going to be, and a choice in the impact we have on ourselves and others. This life is solely experienced and created through our individual eyes, minds, hearts and spirits. So how will you leave this world?...better or worse, for having you in it? A blunt question, I know. But understand that my words are meant with nothing but an immense amount of love for you. I want the best for you and I want you to be the best for yourselves. My intention is to help you think much more deeply about what internal and external balance really means, to clear a path for you, in what can often be a large amount of emotional and internal confusion, and to help to spur you in achieving that balance. We ALL are, and deserve, unconditional love at our cores. Choose to come back to source center and BE that unconditional deserving person in love. It is always attainable and no one is an exception.

I haven't been writing this to make any other point than to show you how important we are to our own state of happiness, peace, acceptance and love. And going even one more day, not doing something about any imbalances you see within yourself, is a wasted opportunity. You have no control over another person but you do have control over yourself and how you experience and interact in this life.

Clear out what no longer serves you in this life and open yourself to balance and to love.

I wish for open, fulfilling, passionate, balanced, happy, successful, FULL lives for all of you out there; even the people that have gone against me. They just haven't been able to comprehend that. And I am putting focus on those adjectives for my own life as well.

With an immense amount of love and peace to you all,

~Amber

Chapter 8

<u>Meaningful Quotes</u>:

I have a huge love and appreciation for reading quotes, as you can see by some of the quotes I have included in this piece. Reading words from various people's lives and works has always been a great help to me throughout my life. So I have decided to include some more quotes here that have spoken to me strongly, while trying to process what was happening in my life. I hope they can speak to you strongly as well.

<u>A sincere "Thank You" to each quoted individual</u>:

"Not until we are lost do we begin to understand ourselves."
~ Henry David Thoreau

"Sometimes people pretend you're a bad person, so they don't feel guilty about the things they did to you." ~Bryant McGill

"One does not become enlightened by imagining figures of light but by making the darkness conscious. The latter procedure, however, is disagreeable and therefore not popular." ~ C.G. Jung

"Every positive change – every jump to a higher level of energy and awareness – involves a rite of passage. Each time to ascend

to a higher rung on the ladder of personal evolution, we must go through a period of discomfort, of initiation. I have never found an exception." ~ Dan Millman

"You can tell a lot about a person by what they choose to see in you." ~ Unknown.

"No matter what you do – stand up for who you are and be honest about your feelings. Even if it seems like you will be crucified for it; even if you think you will not be as successful or as liked – in the end, it's only your honesty that will have mattered." ~Bryant McGill

"The more out of control someone is, the more they try to control others." & ... *"What they hate is their own lack of self-control, so they try to control you. What they despise is your strength. What they hold in utmost contempt is your refusal to be controlled and to accept their lie, that it's your fault."* ~Bryant McGill

"Don't walk behind me; I may not lead. Don't walk in front of me; I may not follow. Just walk beside me and be my friend." ~ A.A. Milne, "Winnie The Pooh"

"The friend who can be silent with us in a moment of despair or

confusion, who can stay with us in an hour of grief and bereavement, who can tolerate not knowing, not curing, not healing and face with us the reality of our powerlessness, that is a friend who cares." ~ Henri J.M. Nouwen

"You didn't make a mistake by loving them. You should never regret loving. You didn't make a mistake by giving them a chance. That's a reason of strength, not shame. You didn't make a mistake by trusting them, believing them, or being there for them. Do you know why? Your actions reflect you. You would do this for anyone that comes your way. It just happened that those were not appreciative of your pure intentions. You didn't make a mistake. The mistake was their choice to make by not respecting and appreciating your beautiful heart." ~ Mandy Hale

"I have decided to stick to love...hate is too great a burden to bear." ~ Martin Luther King

"I am grateful to those who have betrayed me...they thought they were just stabbing me in the back, but they were also cutting me free from their poisonous life." ~ Steve Maraboli

"No matter how educated, talented, rich or cool you believe you are, how you treat people ultimately tells all. Integrity is everything." ~ Unknown

"Don't ask me to apologize for holding up a mirror. If you don't like what it's reflecting, take accountability and change it." ~ Steve Maraboli

"Your only work is to love yourself, value yourself and embody this truth of self-worth and self-love so that you can be love in action. That is true service, to yourself and to those who surround you." ~ Anita Moorjani

"Do not let the behavior of others destroy your inner peace." ~ Dalai Lama XIV

"I find the best way to love someone is not to change them, but instead, to help them reveal the greatest version of themselves." ~ Steve Maraboli

"Violence never brings permanent peace. It solves no social problem: it merely creates new and more complicated ones. Violence is impractical because it is a descending spiral ending in destruction for all. It is immoral because it seeks to humiliate the opponent rather than win his understanding: it seeks to annihilate rather than convert. Violence is immoral because it thrives on hatred rather than love. It destroys community and makes brotherhood impossible. It leaves society in monologue rather than dialogue. Violence ends up defeating itself. It creates

bitterness in the survivors and brutality in the destroyers." ~
Martin Luther King

"Recognize that what you think about expands. Monitor your
inner dialogue and match your thoughts to what you want and
what you intend to create." ~ Wayne Dyer

"We can easily forgive a child who is afraid of the dark; the real
tragedy of life is when men are afraid of the light." ~ Plato

"I shall serve as a mirror for you, because I care for you. I would
like to let you finally see what has been hidden from your
searchingly hungry gaze: your red heart." ~ Waylon Lewis

"Your task is not to seek love, but merely to seek and find all of
the barriers within yourself that you have built against it." ~
Rumi

~

We All

There is nothing more important than our souls.

Nothing we should care about more,

Or pay attention to more.

Yours and mine,

Ours and theirs,

It really is all the same.

A revolving door...

We are ALL on this planet for just a blink of time in this life.

We can choose to be a part of the collective answer,

Or a part of the cause of universal strife.

So choose wisely:

Fear or Love?

Will you be like the Hammer?

Or will you be like the Dove?

All of our decisions, actions and reactions

fall into this simply stated, yet widely varying meaningful range.

It is true that the littlest act of kindness

can sometimes create the hugest ripple of positive change.

We may not even know the effect that we have,

But that doesn't make it any less true.

So I am choosing Love;

For myself and for you.

I am another flawed Human Being;

But I vow to audit my responses and try to react from what is true,

To try to do what is best;

Both for myself and for the collective too.

A life-long goal.

It can be difficult

But yet a goal of utmost necessity.

I challenge you all,

To put fear, pride and ego aside…

As best you can.

Choose LOVE.

And join me.

~ Amber Howard

ABOUT THE AUTHOR

Amber Howard was born and raised in San Jose, CA and currently resides in Southern California. Compelled by an internal necessity for creativity and movement, some of her projects have included photography, modeling, fitness training, acting, voice-over, dancing, singing and writing. She has previously published the book, "Fallen: A Book Of Poetry". Always a deeply reflective and emotionally sensitive individual, she feels a great pull to use these personal traits to nurture and to spread deeper understanding, compassion and universal love.